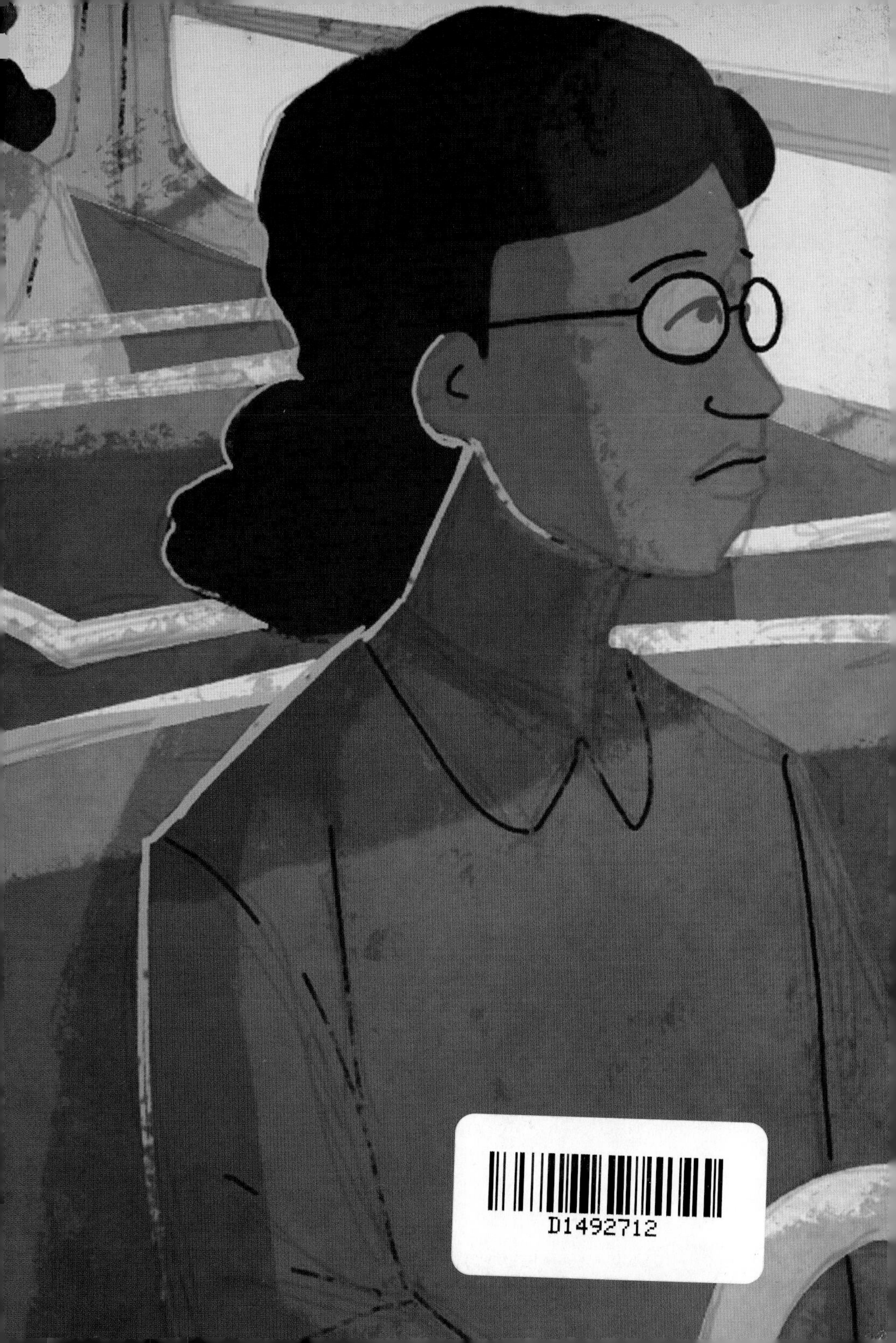

© 2021 Sunbird Books, an imprint of Phoenix International Publications, Inc.
8501 West Higgins Road   59 Gloucester Place
Chicago, Illinois 60631   London W1U 8JJ

www.sunbirdkidsbooks.com

Sunbird Books and the colophon are trademarks of Phoenix International Publications, Inc.

ISBN: 978-1-5037-5294-8 Printed in China

The art for this book was created digitally. Text set in Scotty O.

IT'S HER STORY
ROSA PARKS

Written by Lauren Burke
Illustrated by Shane Clester

sunbird books

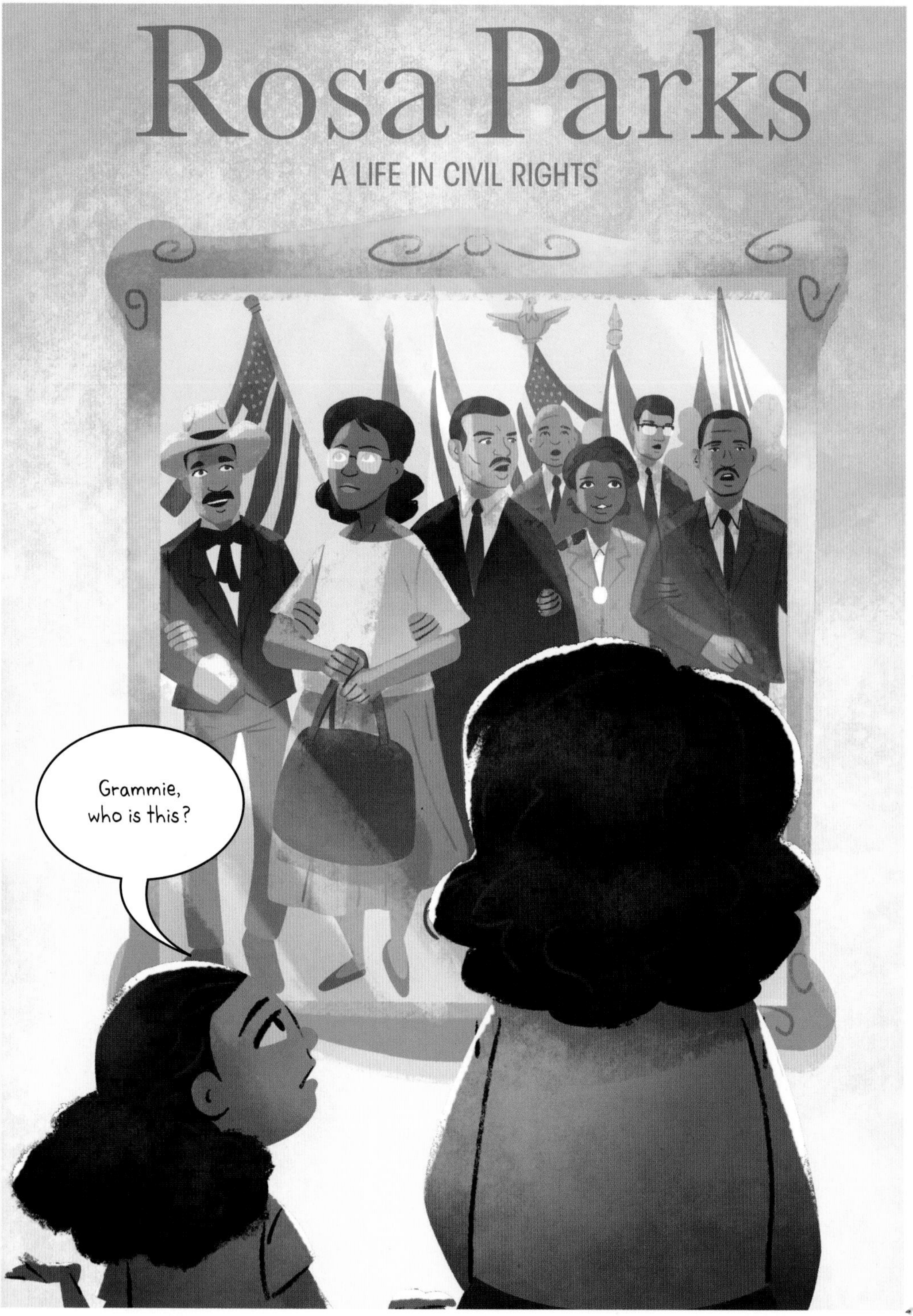
Rosa Parks
A LIFE IN CIVIL RIGHTS
Grammie,
who is this?

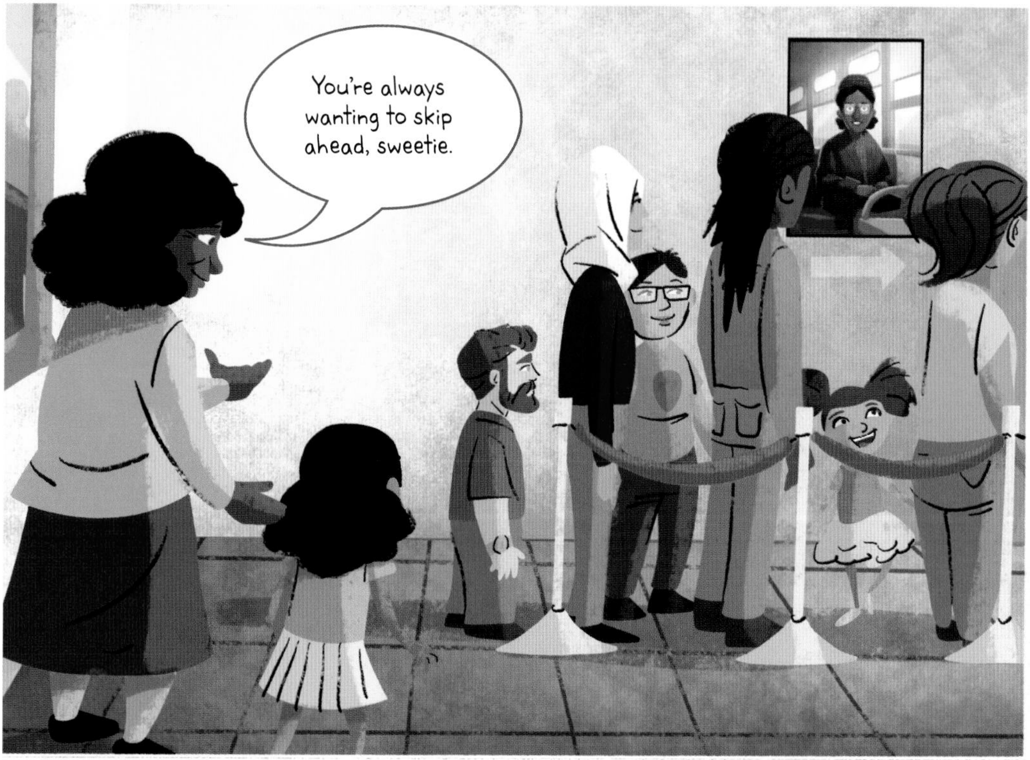
You're always wanting to skip ahead, sweetie.

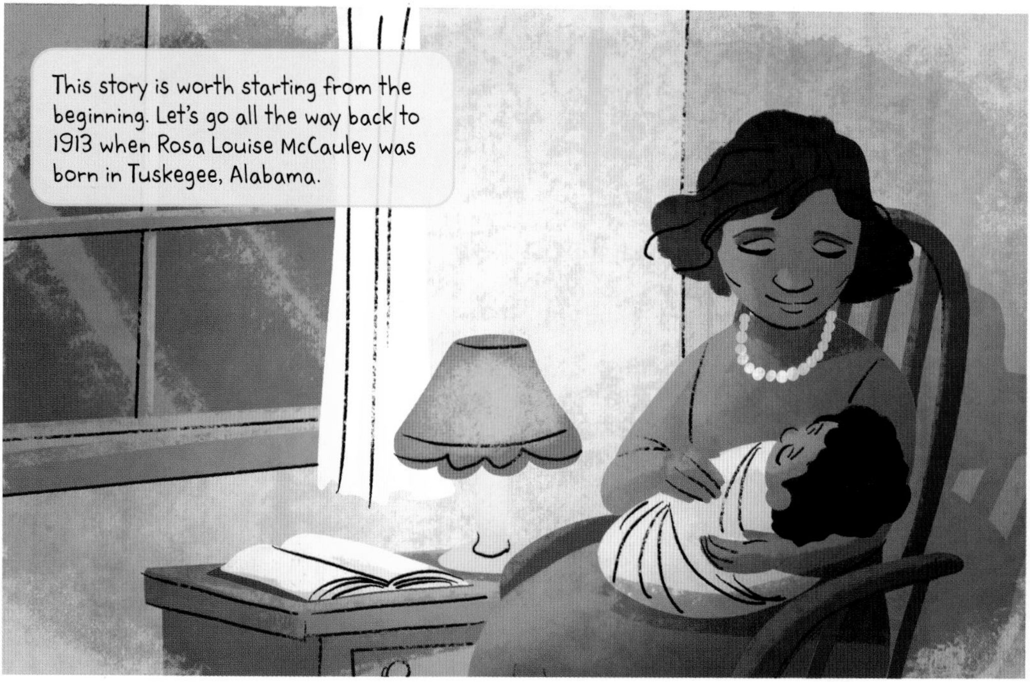
This story is worth starting from the beginning. Let's go all the way back to 1913 when Rosa Louise McCauley was born in Tuskegee, Alabama.

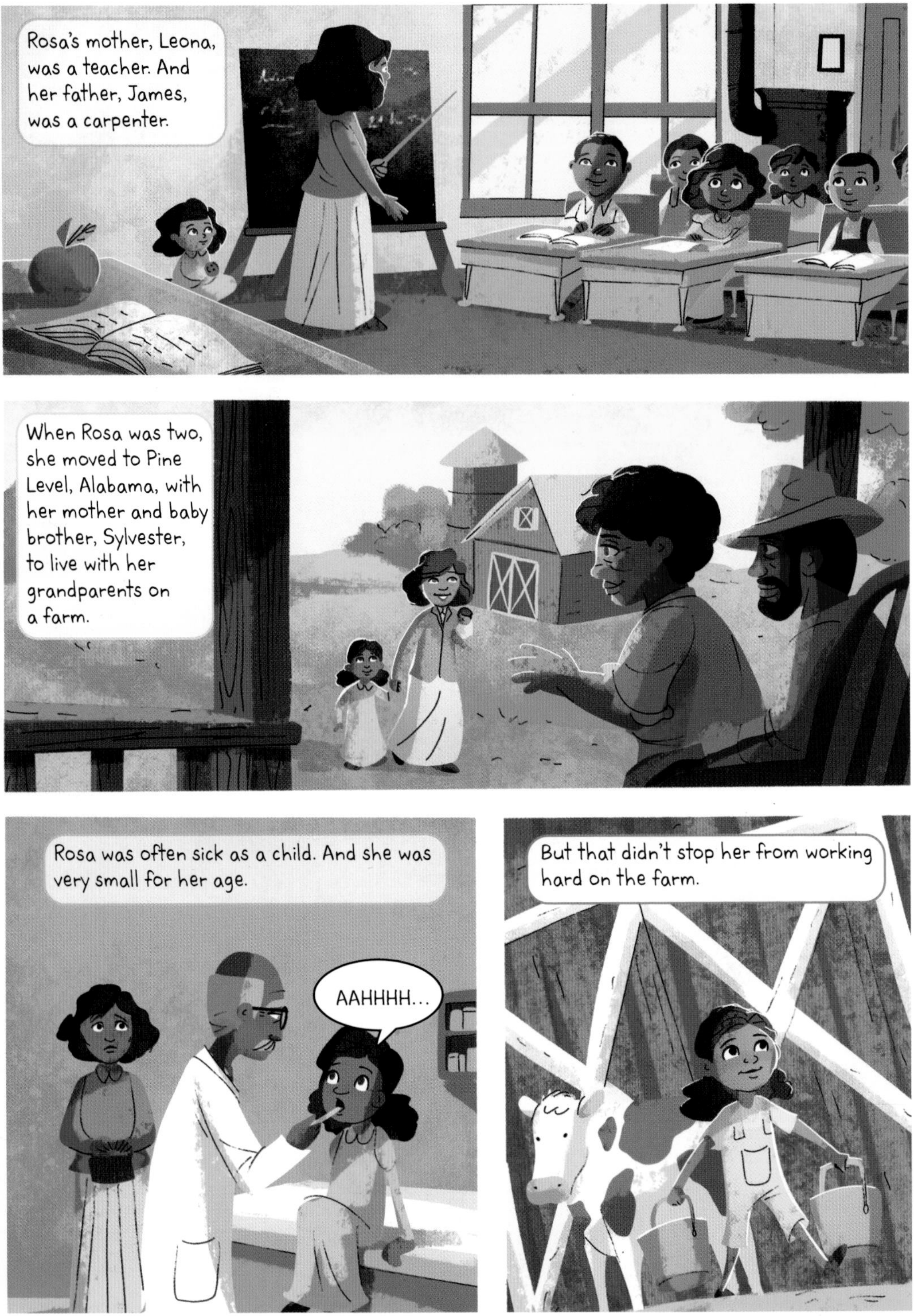
Rosa's mother, Leona, was a teacher. And her father, James, was a carpenter.
When Rosa was two, she moved to Pine Level, Alabama, with her mother and baby brother, Sylvester, to live with her grandparents on a farm.
Rosa was often sick as a child. And she was very small for her age.
AAHHHH...
But that didn't stop her from working hard on the farm.

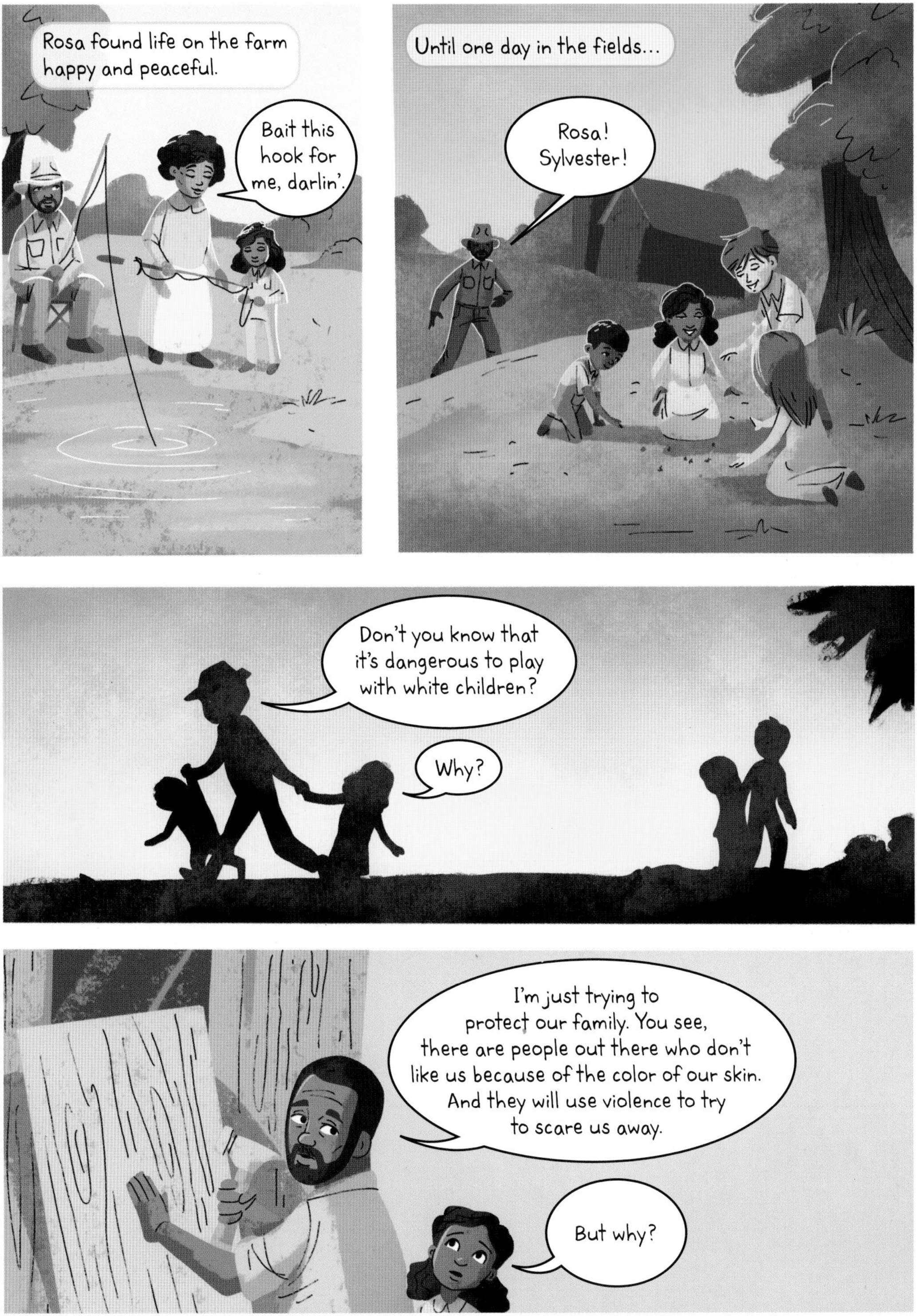

Rosa found life on the farm happy and peaceful.
Bait this hook for me, darlin'.
Until one day in the fields...
Rosa! Sylvester!
Don't you know that it's dangerous to play with white children?
Why?
I'm just trying to protect our family. You see, there are people out there who don't like us because of the color of our skin. And they will use violence to try to scare us away.
But why?

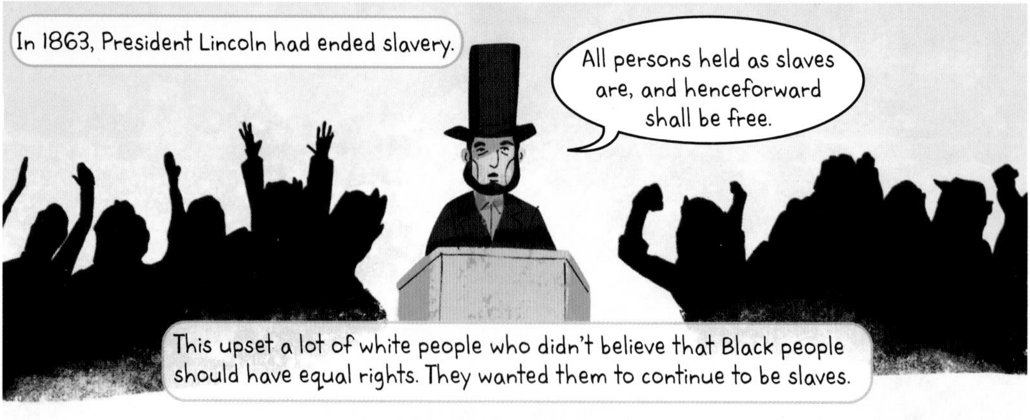
In 1863, President Lincoln had ended slavery.
All persons held as slaves are, and henceforward shall be free.
This upset a lot of white people who didn't believe that Black people should have equal rights. They wanted them to continue to be slaves.

Starting in 1870, laws were made to keep the races separate.

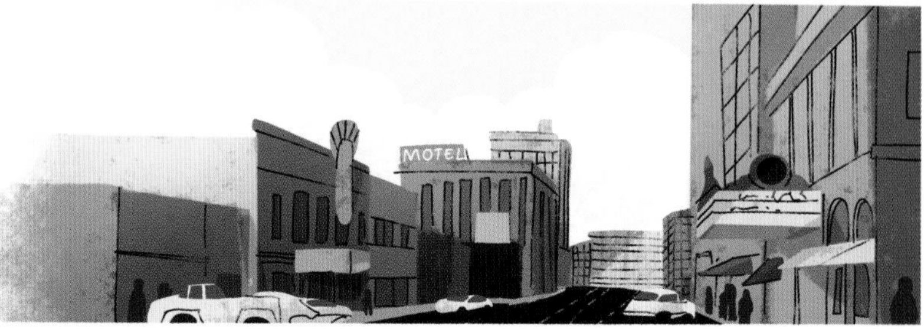
MOTEL

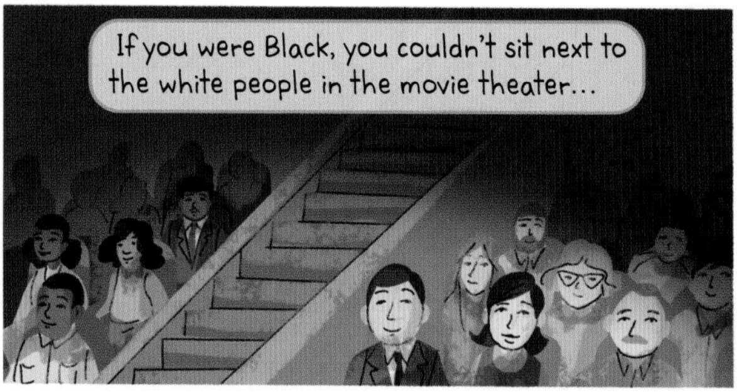
If you were Black, you couldn't sit next to the white people in the movie theater...

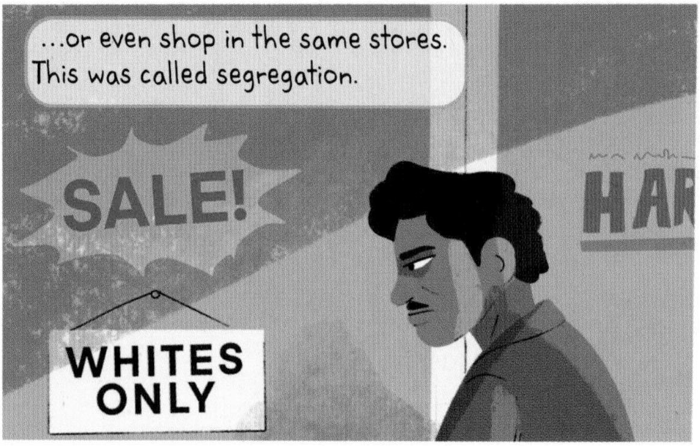
...or even shop in the same stores. This was called segregation.
SALE!
HAR
WHITES ONLY

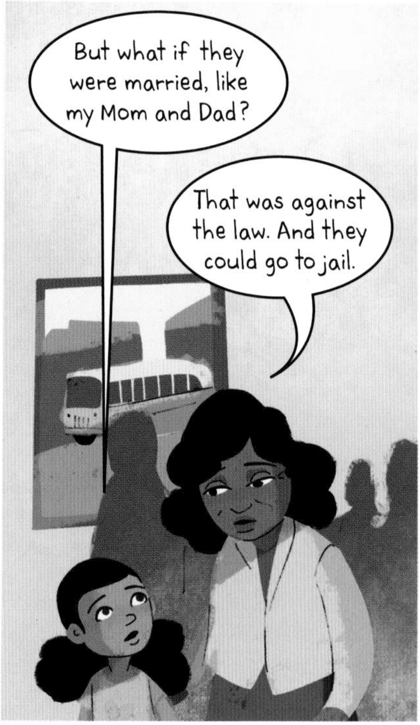
But what if they were married, like my Mom and Dad?
That was against the law. And they could go to jail.

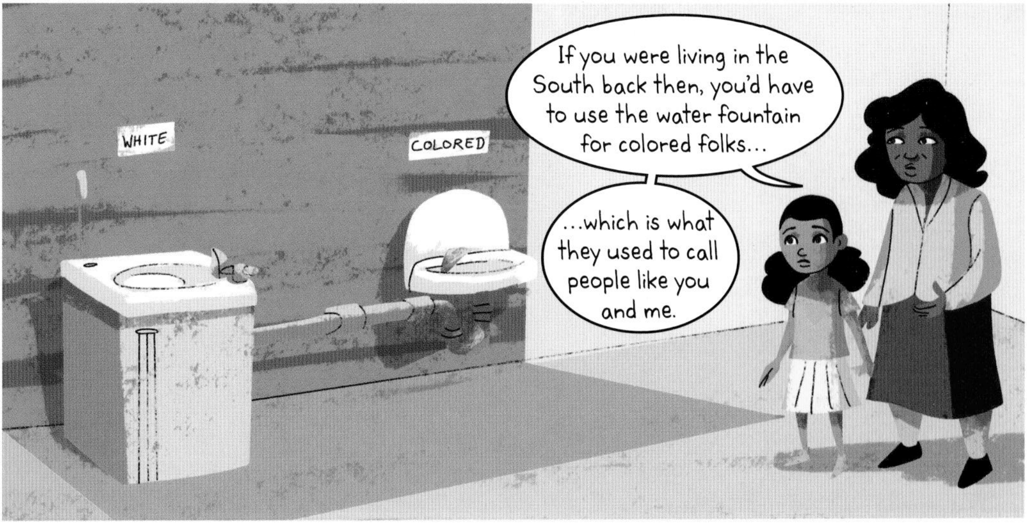
WHITE
COLORED
If you were living in the South back then, you'd have to use the water fountain for colored folks...
...which is what they used to call people like you and me.

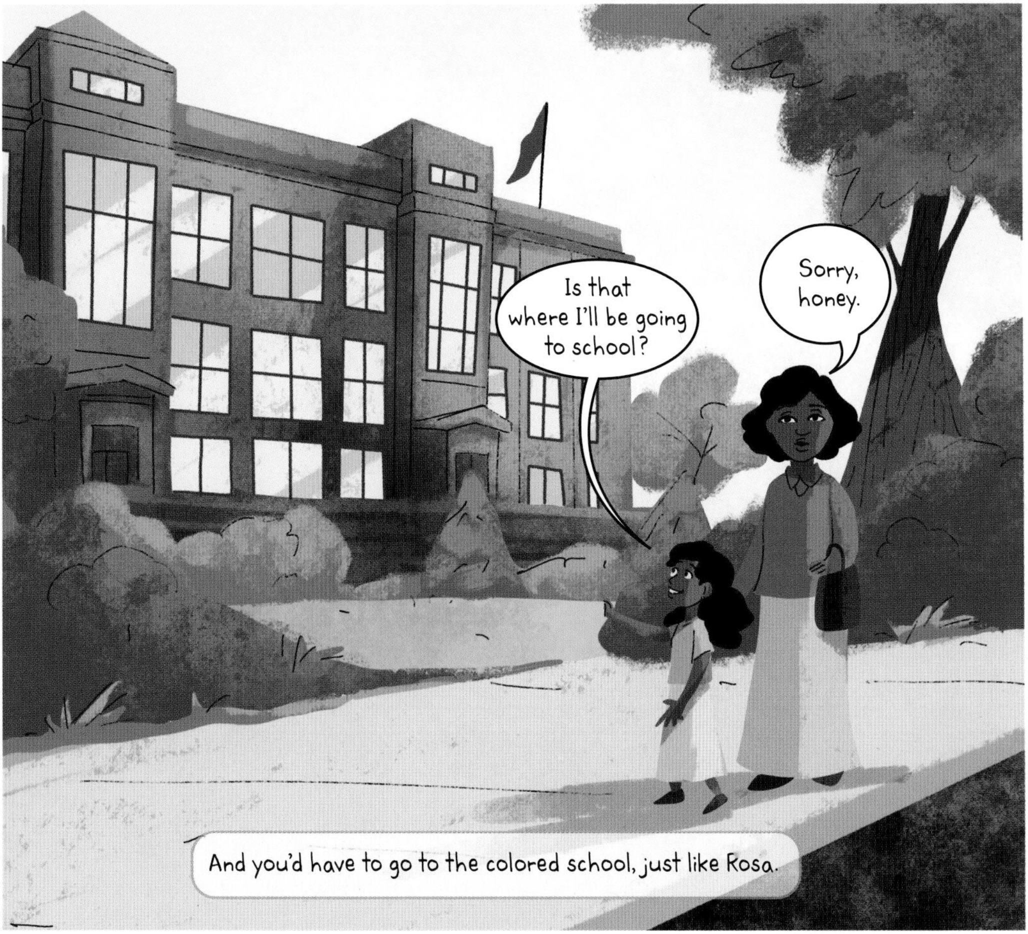
Is that where I'll be going to school?
Sorry, honey.
And you'd have to go to the colored school, just like Rosa.

In those days, white children would go to school for nine months out of the year, while Black children went to school for only five months.

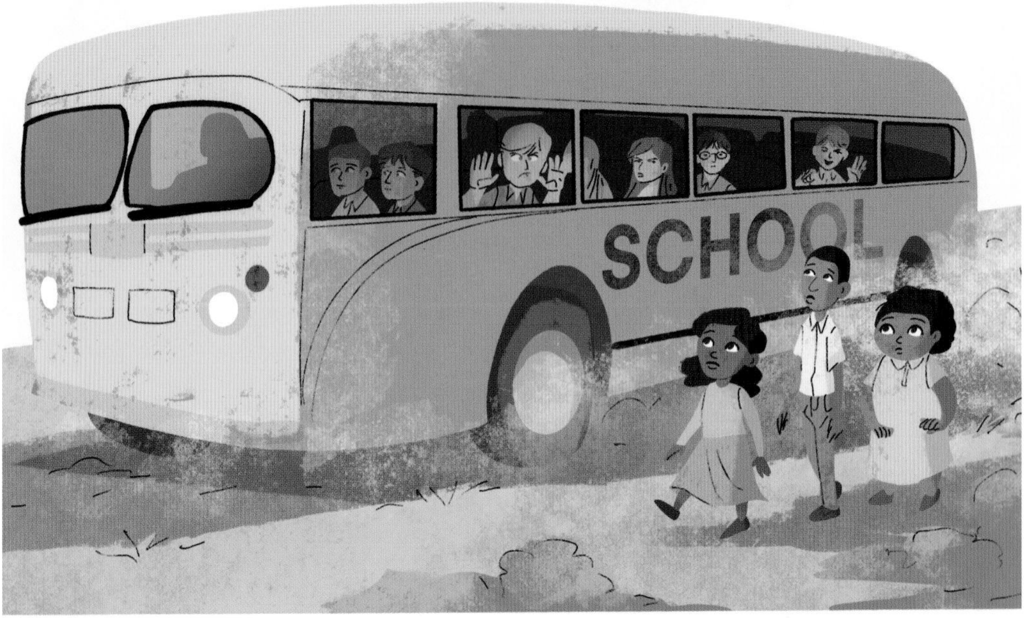
SCHOOL

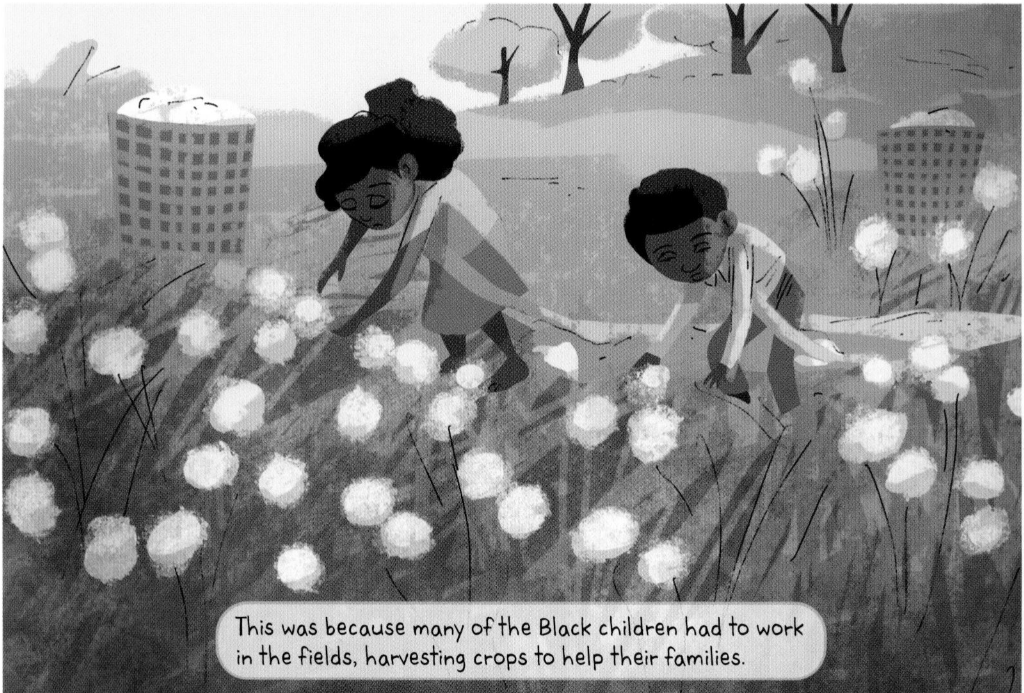
This was because many of the Black children had to work in the fields, harvesting crops to help their families.

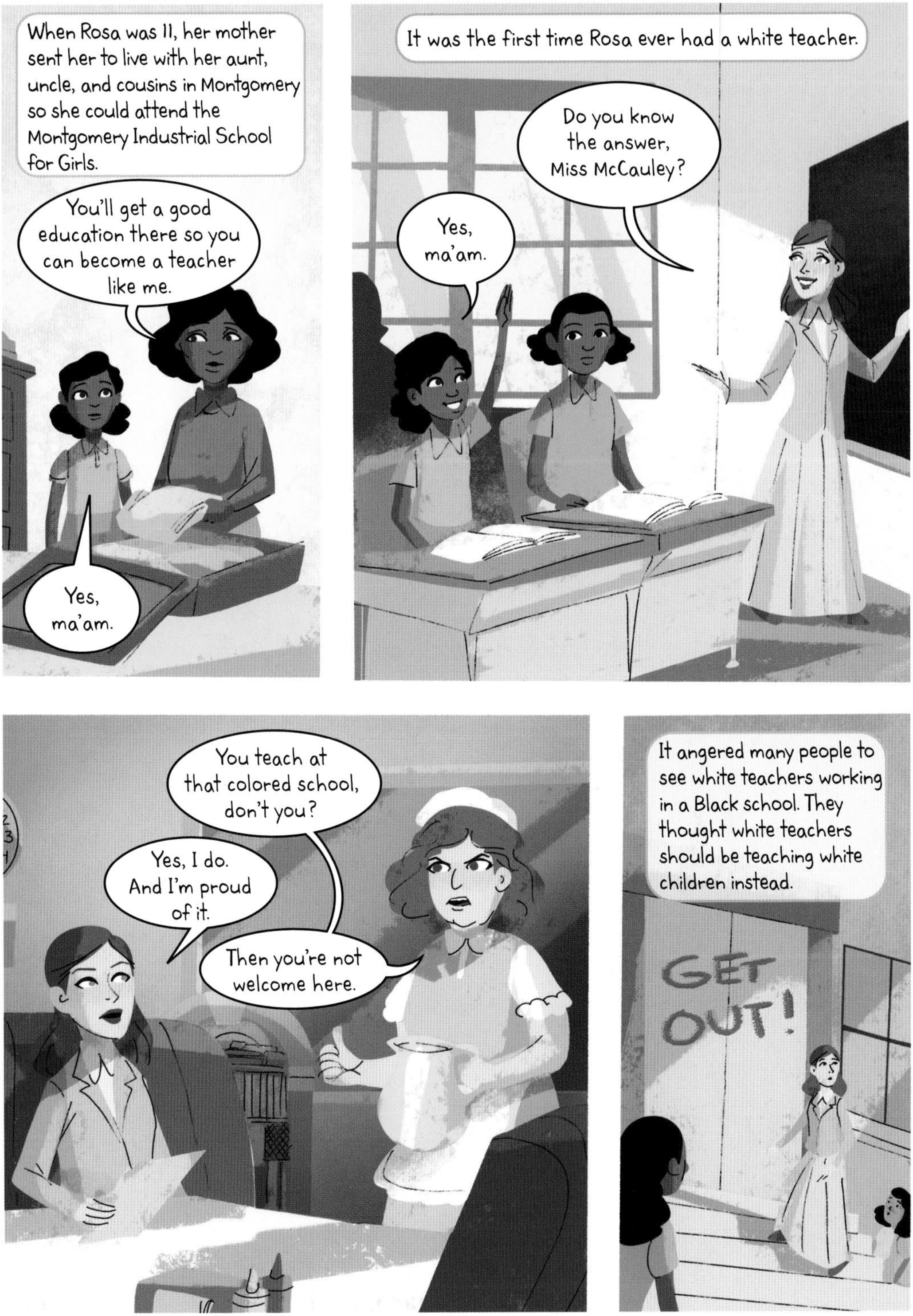

When Rosa was 11, her mother sent her to live with her aunt, uncle, and cousins in Montgomery so she could attend the Montgomery Industrial School for Girls.
You'll get a good education there so you can become a teacher like me.
Yes, ma'am.
It was the first time Rosa ever had a white teacher.
Do you know the answer, Miss McCauley?
Yes, ma'am.
You teach at that colored school, don't you?
Yes, I do. And I'm proud of it.
Then you're not welcome here.
It angered many people to see white teachers working in a Black school. They thought white teachers should be teaching white children instead.
GET OUT!

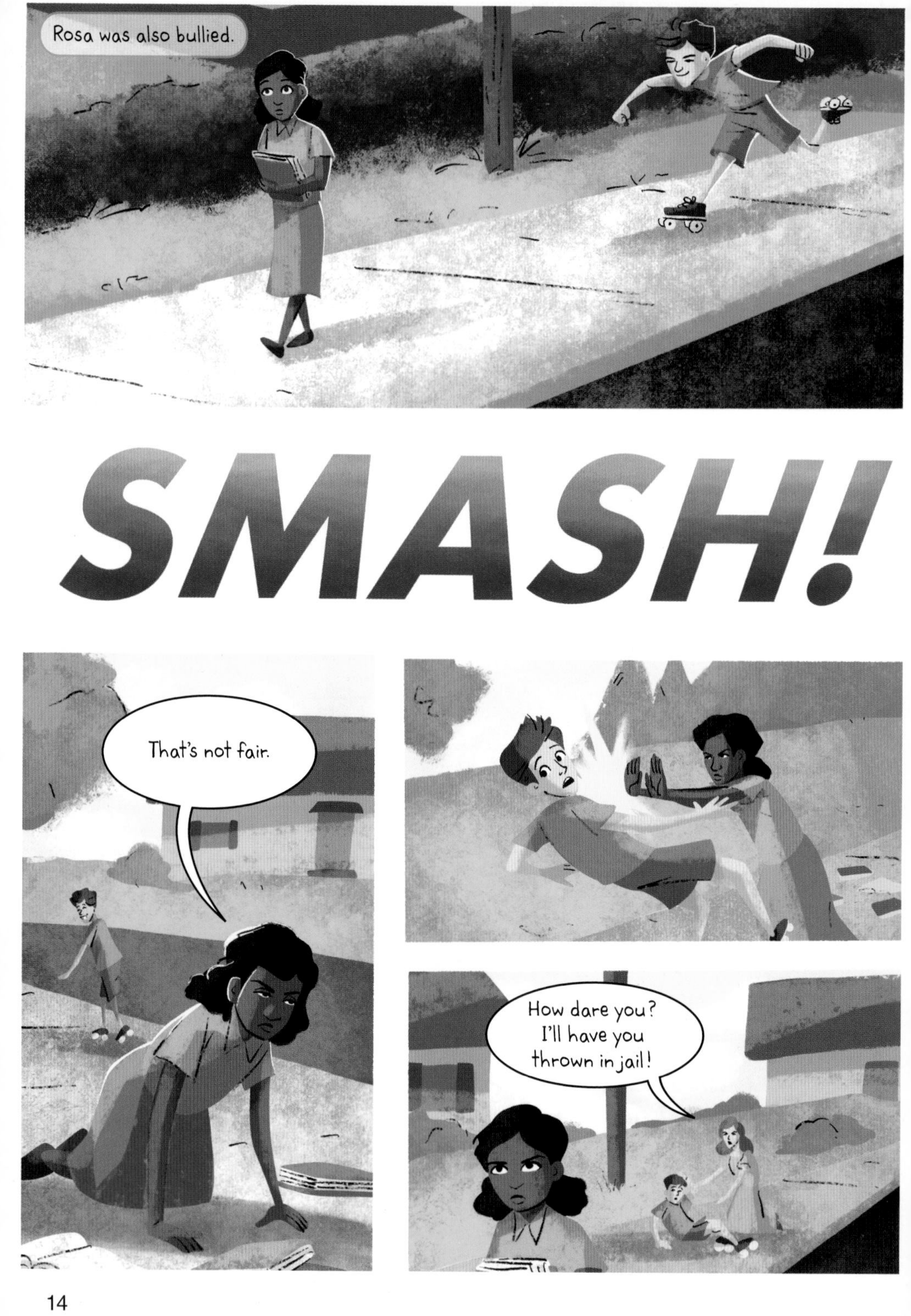
Rosa was also bullied.
SMASH!
That's not fair.
How dare you? I'll have you thrown in jail!

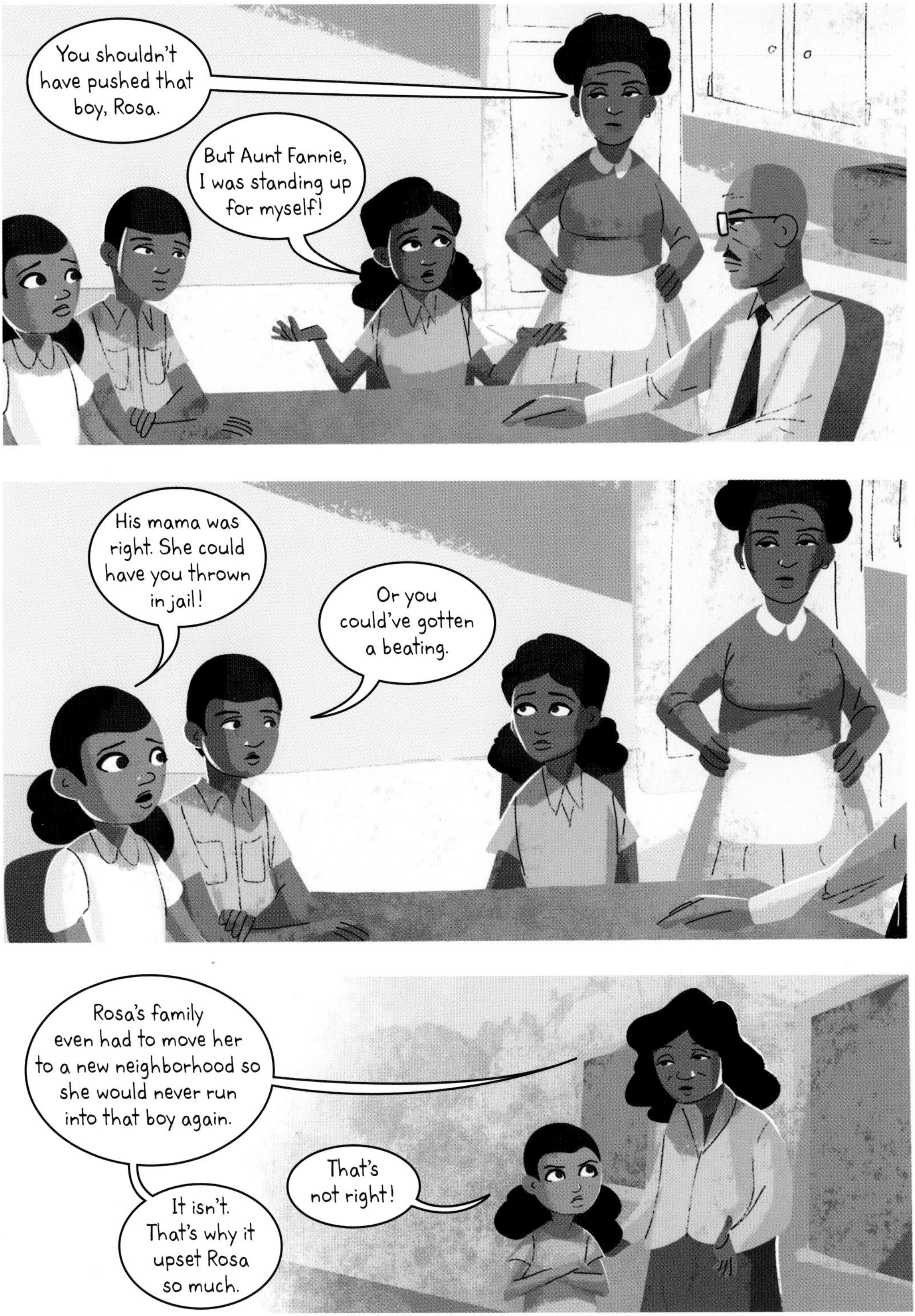
You shouldn't have pushed that boy, Rosa.
But Aunt Fannie, I was standing up for myself!
His mama was right. She could have you thrown in jail!
Or you could've gotten a beating.
Rosa's family even had to move her to a new neighborhood so she would never run into that boy again.
That's not right!
It isn't. That's why it upset Rosa so much.

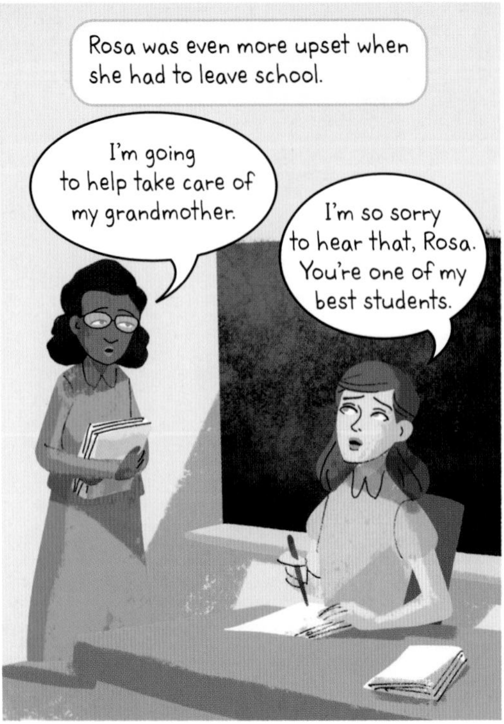
Rosa was even more upset when she had to leave school.
I'm going to help take care of my grandmother.
I'm so sorry to hear that, Rosa. You're one of my best students.

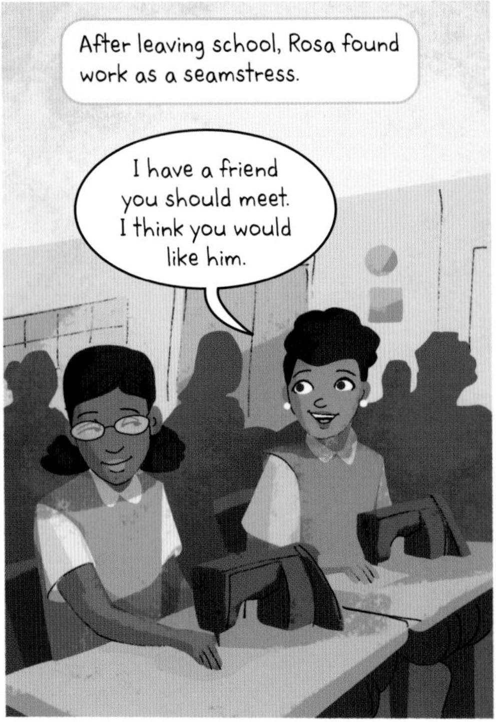
After leaving school, Rosa found work as a seamstress.
I have a friend you should meet. I think you would like him.

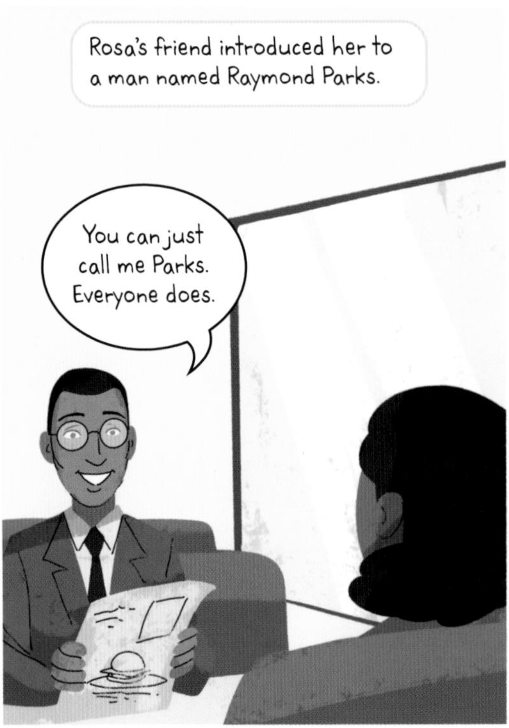
Rosa's friend introduced her to a man named Raymond Parks.
You can just call me Parks. Everyone does.

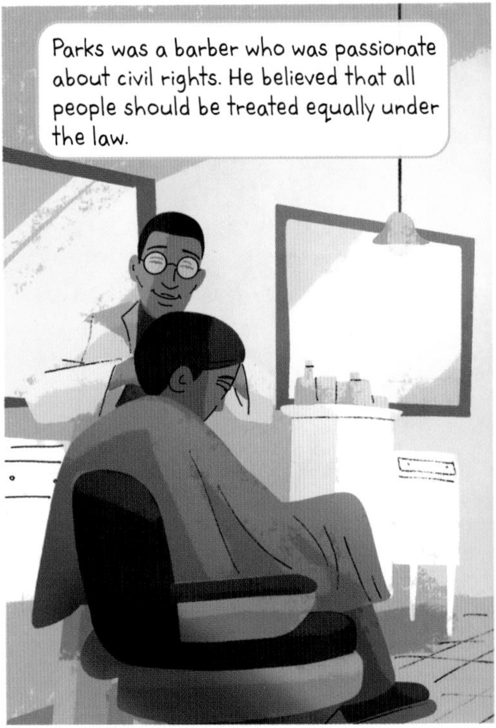
Parks was a barber who was passionate about civil rights. He believed that all people should be treated equally under the law.

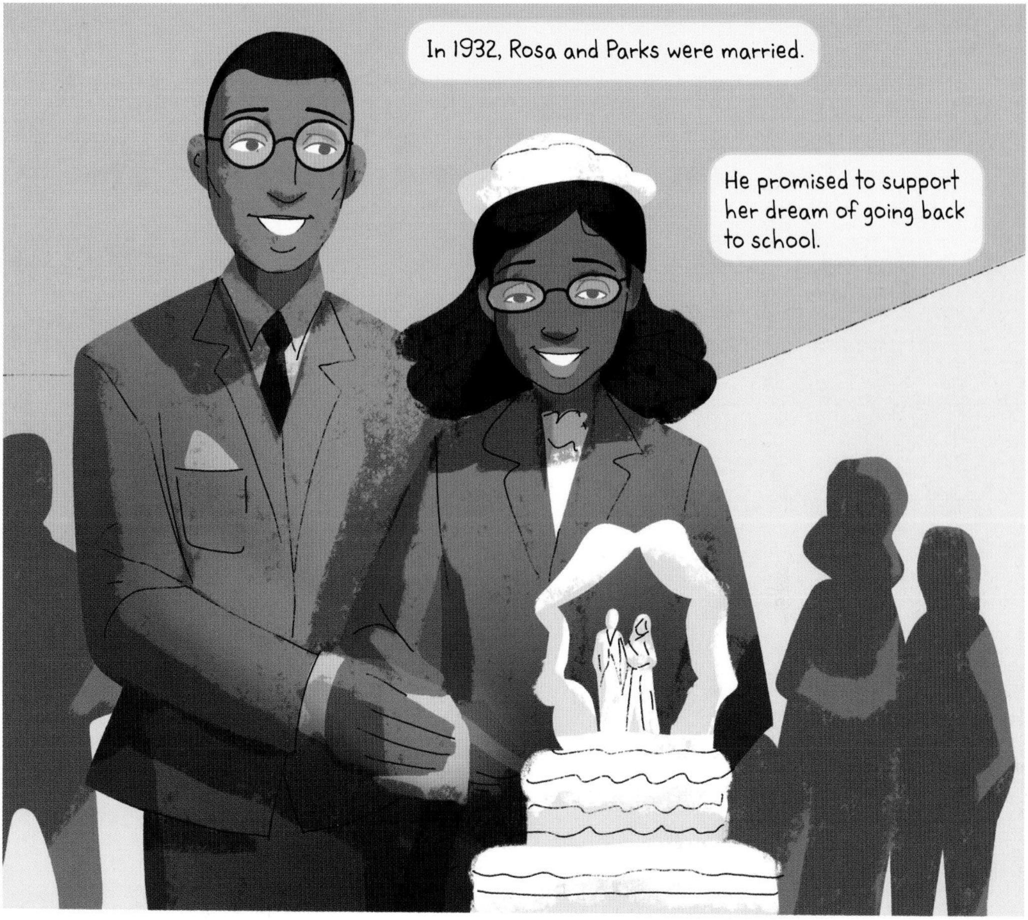
In 1932, Rosa and Parks were married.
He promised to support her dream of going back to school.

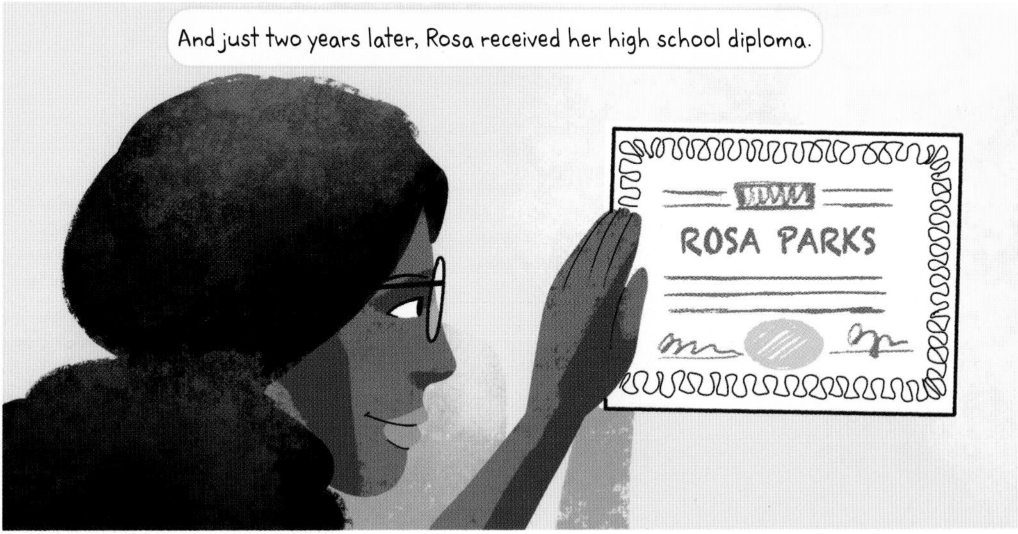
And just two years later, Rosa received her high school diploma.
ROSA PARKS

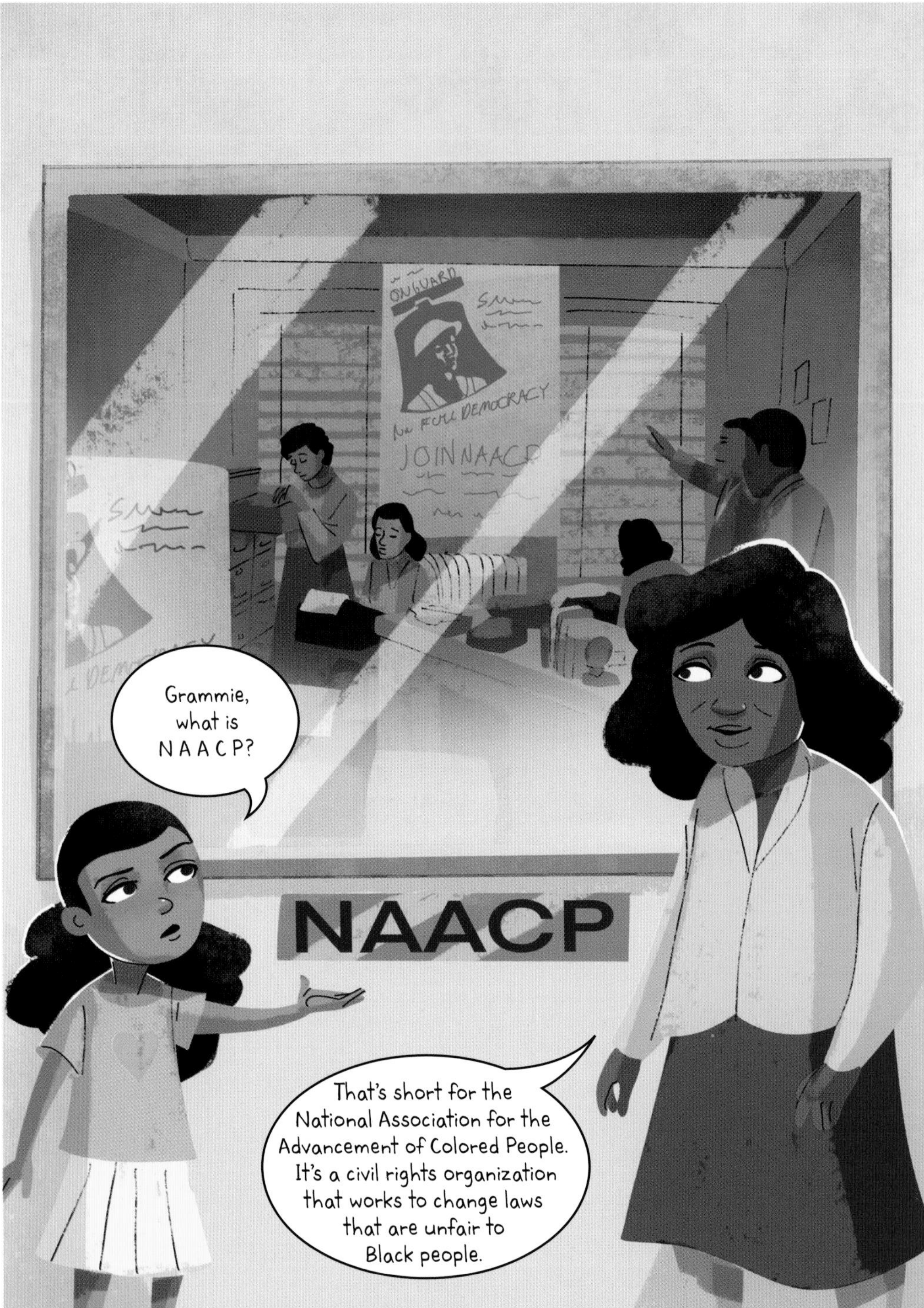
ONGUARD
FULL DEMOCRACY
JOIN NAACP
Grammie, what is NAACP?
NAACP
That's short for the National Association for the Advancement of Colored People. It's a civil rights organization that works to change laws that are unfair to Black people.

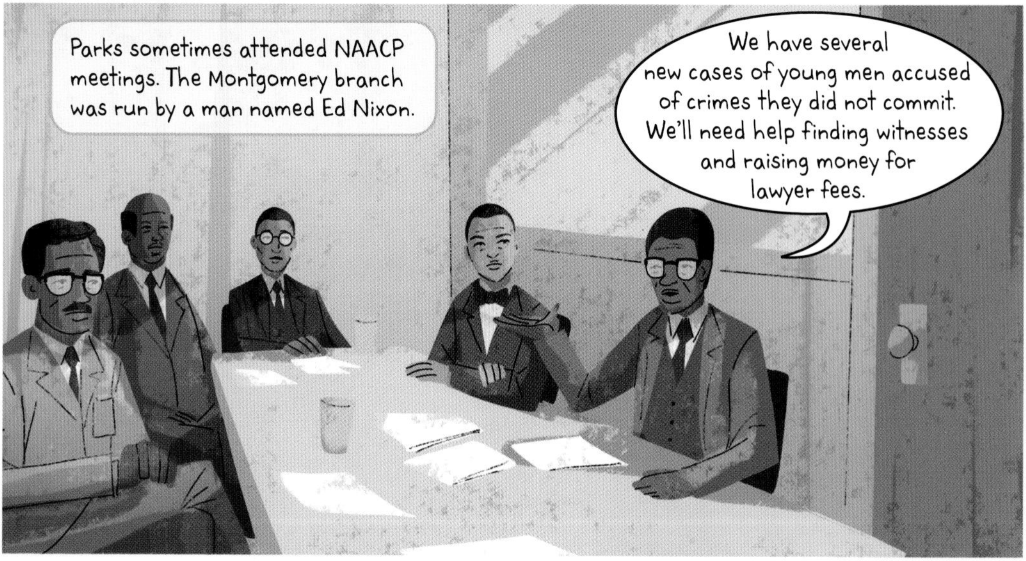
Parks sometimes attended NAACP meetings. The Montgomery branch was run by a man named Ed Nixon.
We have several new cases of young men accused of crimes they did not commit. We'll need help finding witnesses and raising money for lawyer fees.

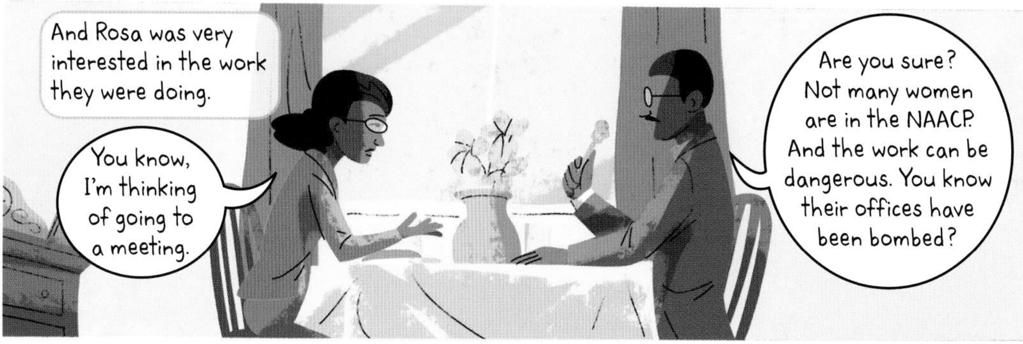
And Rosa was very interested in the work they were doing.
You know, I'm thinking of going to a meeting.
Are you sure? Not many women are in the NAACP. And the work can be dangerous. You know their offices have been bombed?

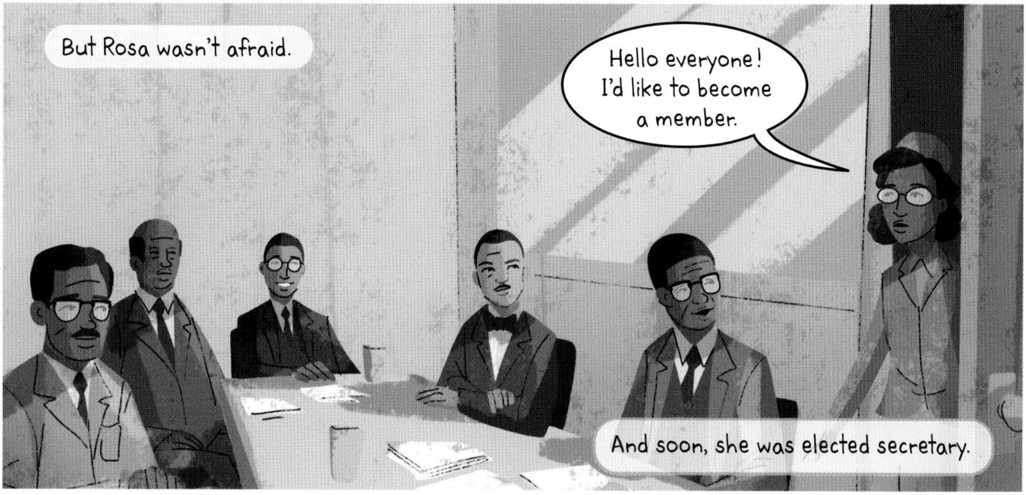
But Rosa wasn't afraid.
Hello everyone! I'd like to become a member.
And soon, she was elected secretary.

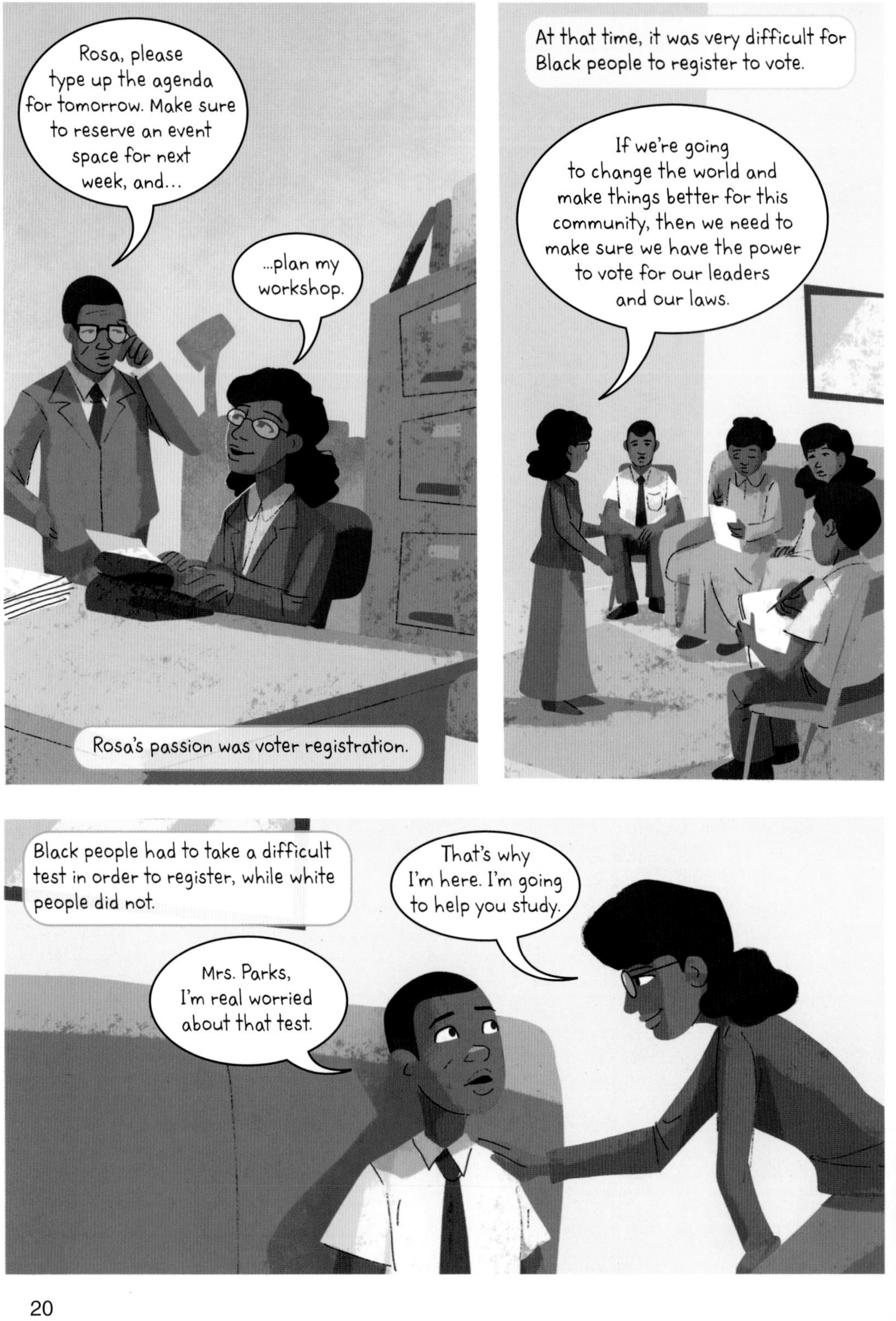
Rosa, please type up the agenda for tomorrow. Make sure to reserve an event space for next week, and...
...plan my workshop.
Rosa's passion was voter registration.
At that time, it was very difficult for Black people to register to vote.
If we're going to change the world and make things better for this community, then we need to make sure we have the power to vote for our leaders and our laws.
Black people had to take a difficult test in order to register, while white people did not.
That's why I'm here. I'm going to help you study.
Mrs. Parks, I'm real worried about that test.

I'll be home late tonight, so you can go ahead and eat dinner without me!

Another crazy day, huh?

Shouldn't you be getting on home?

Yes, sir. Just making sure this last stitch is perfect.

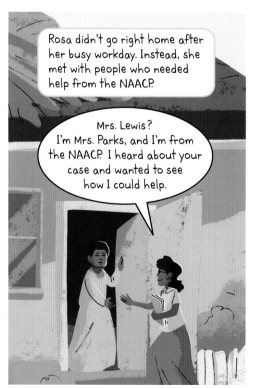

Rosa didn't go right home after her busy workday. Instead, she met with people who needed help from the NAACP.

Mrs. Lewis? I'm Mrs. Parks, and I'm from the NAACP. I heard about your case and wanted to see how I could help.

CLICK-CLICK-CLACKITY-CLACK-CLACK-CLICK-CLICK-CLICK-CLICK-CLACK-CLACK...

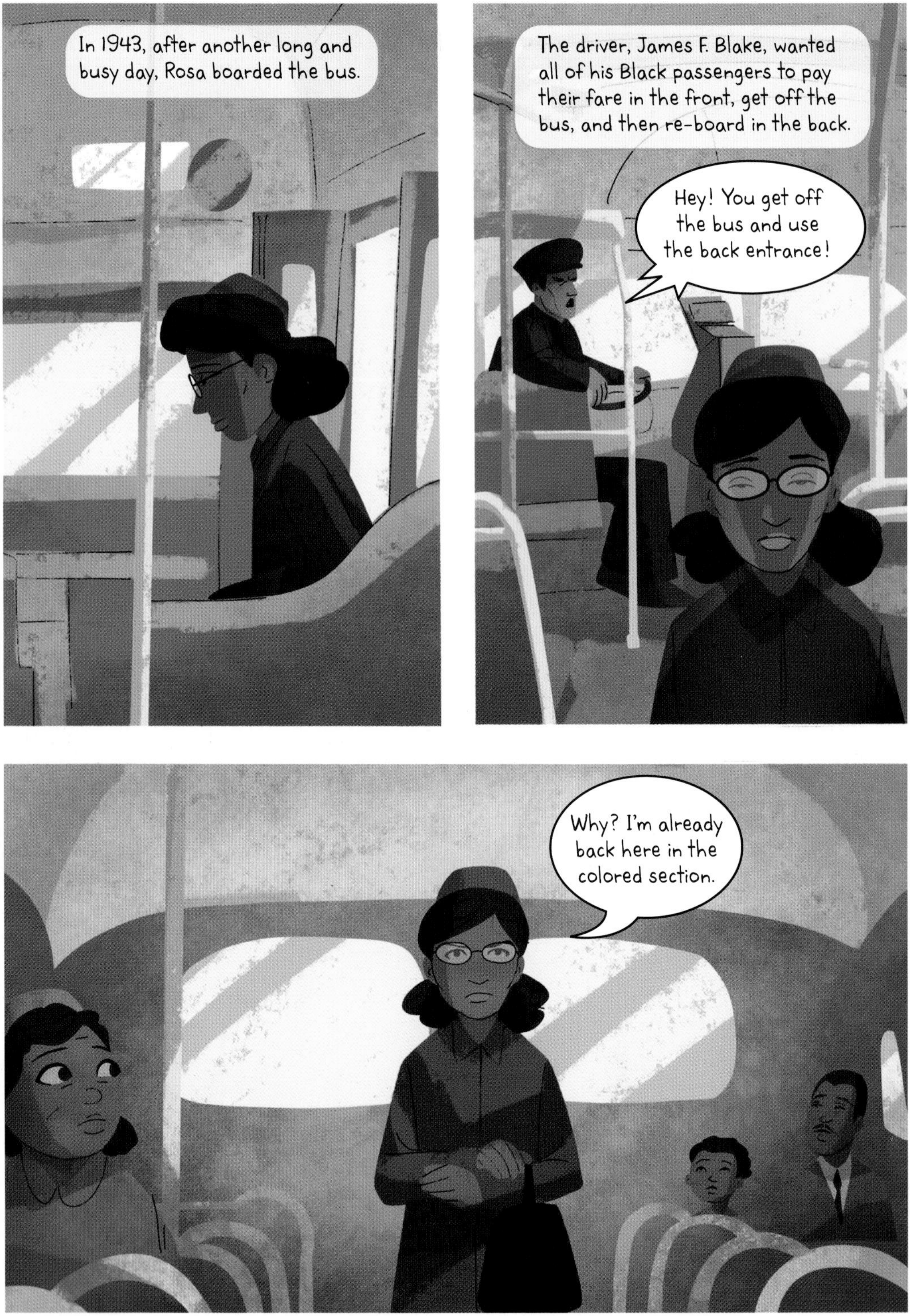
In 1943, after another long and busy day, Rosa boarded the bus.
The driver, James F. Blake, wanted all of his Black passengers to pay their fare in the front, get off the bus, and then re-board in the back.
Hey! You get off the bus and use the back entrance!
Why? I'm already back here in the colored section.

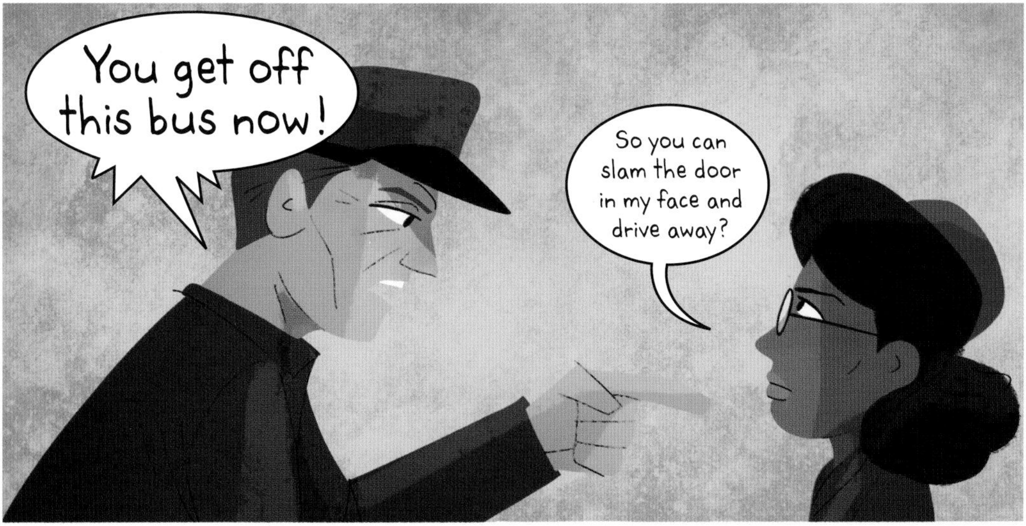
You get off this bus now!
So you can slam the door in my face and drive away?

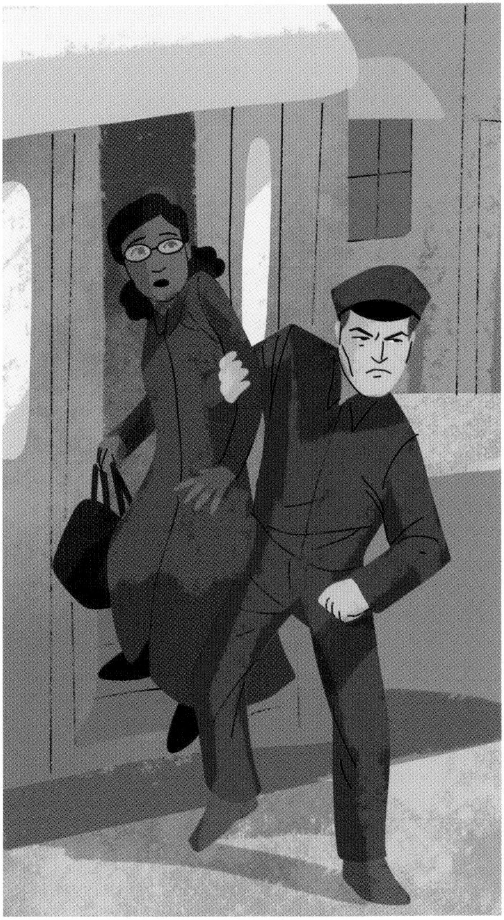

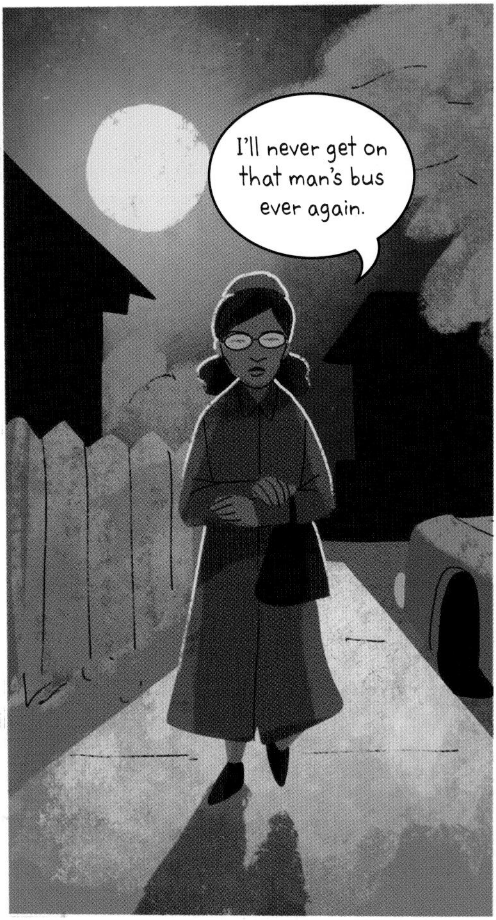
I'll never get on that man's bus ever again.

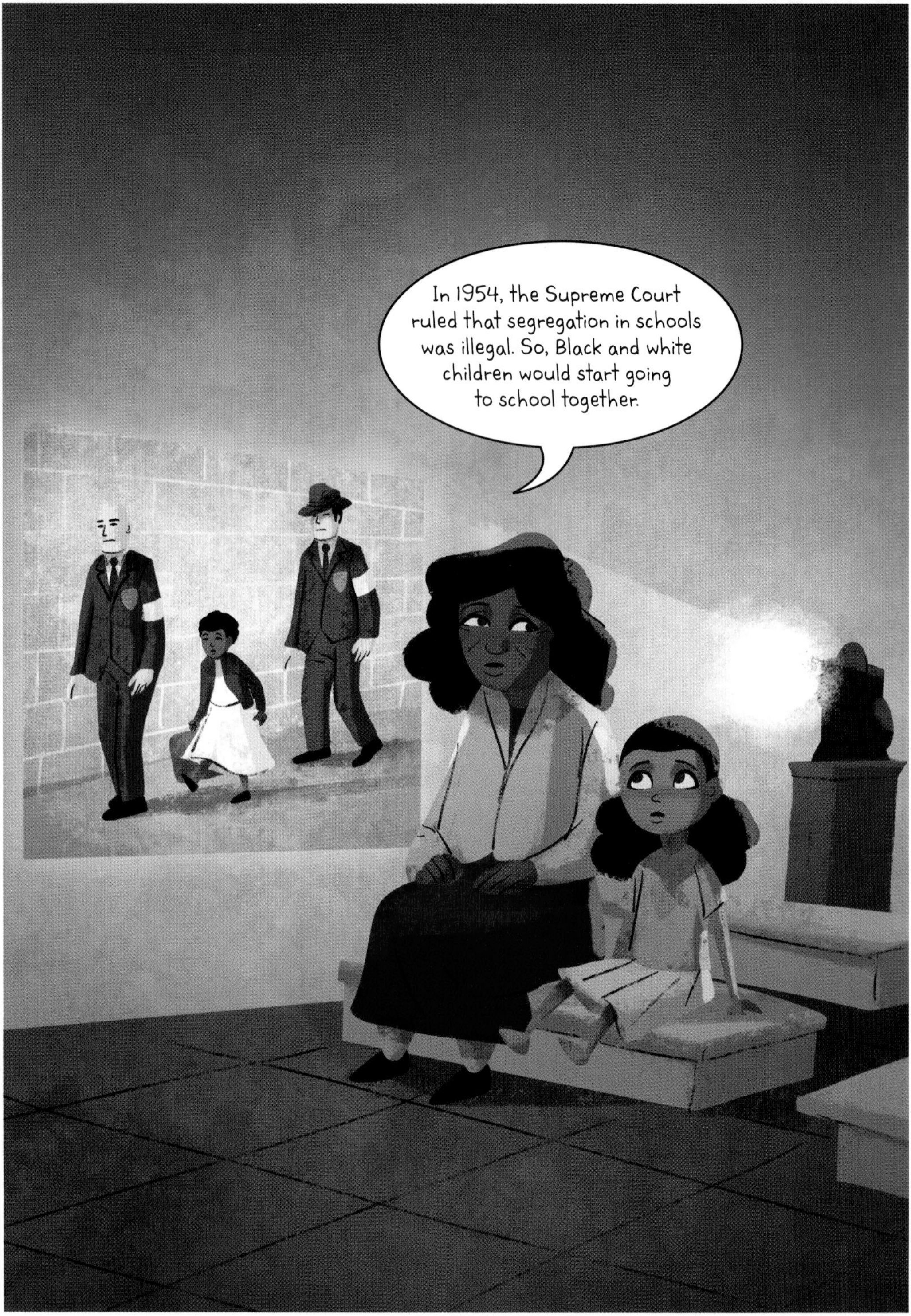
In 1954, the Supreme Court ruled that segregation in schools was illegal. So, Black and white children would start going to school together.

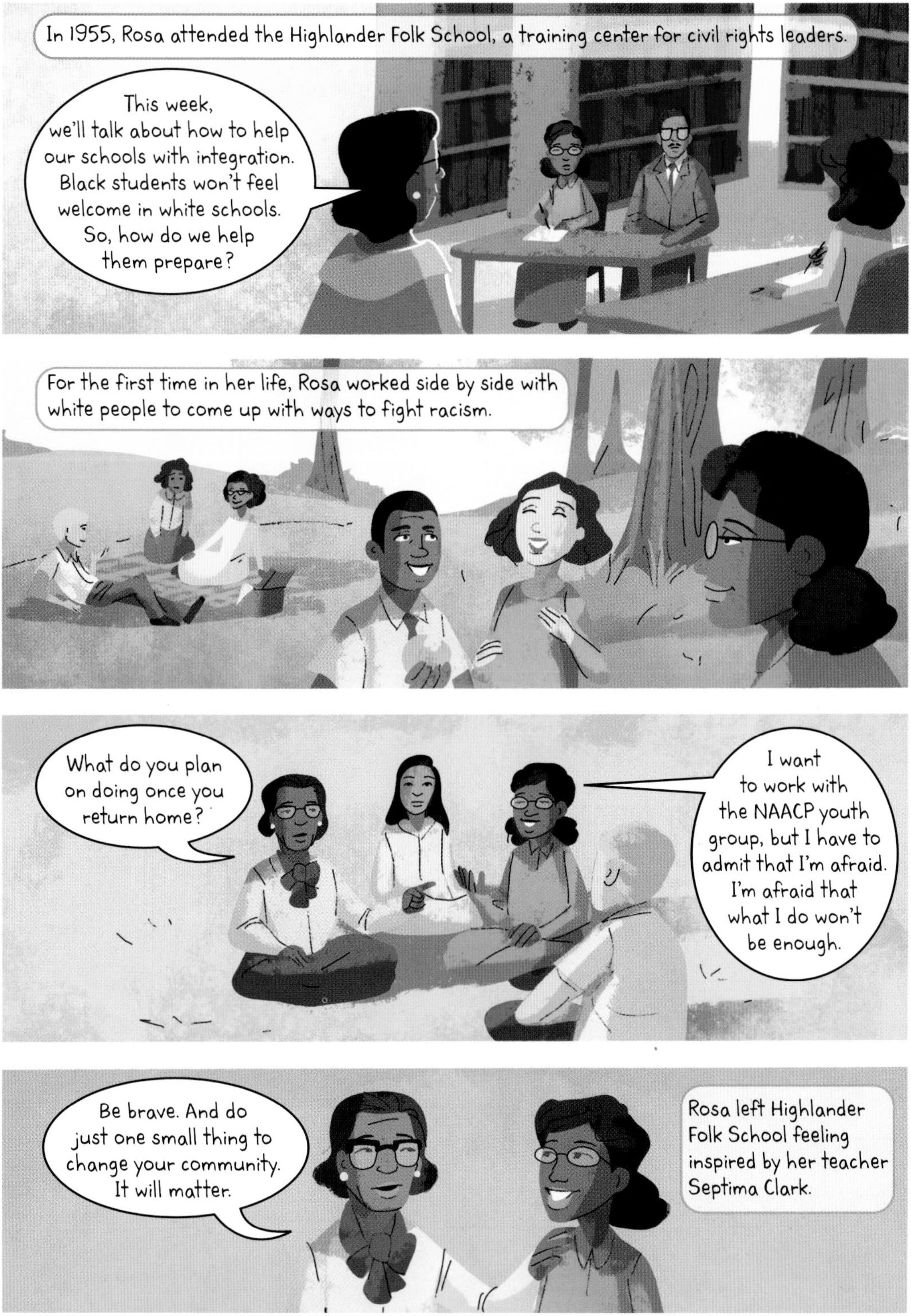
In 1955, Rosa attended the Highlander Folk School, a training center for civil rights leaders.
This week, we'll talk about how to help our schools with integration. Black students won't feel welcome in white schools. So, how do we help them prepare?
For the first time in her life, Rosa worked side by side with white people to come up with ways to fight racism.
What do you plan on doing once you return home?
I want to work with the NAACP youth group, but I have to admit that I'm afraid. I'm afraid that what I do won't be enough.
Be brave. And do just one small thing to change your community. It will matter.
Rosa left Highlander Folk School feeling inspired by her teacher Septima Clark.

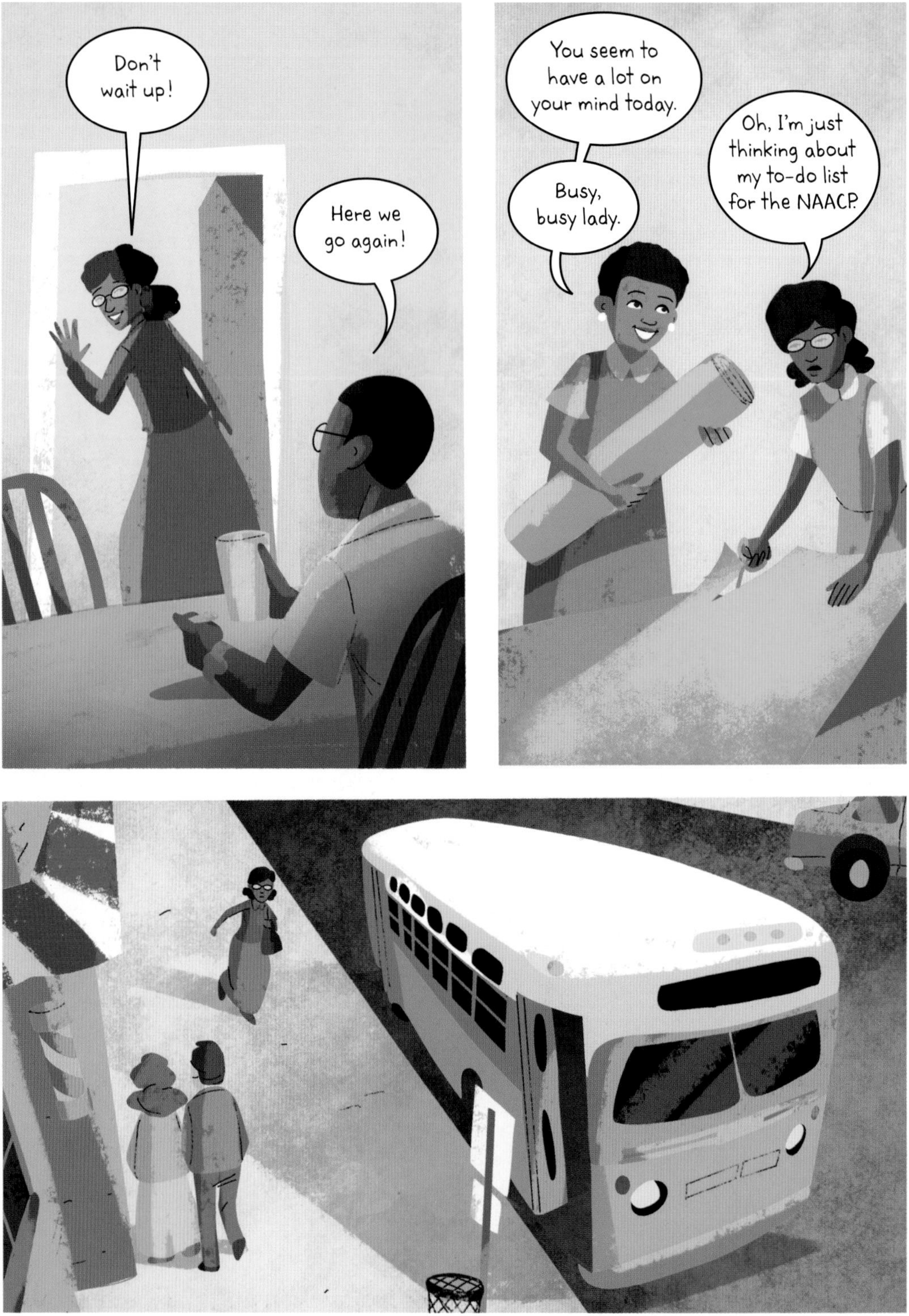
Don't wait up!
Here we go again!
You seem to have a lot on your mind today.
Busy, busy lady.
Oh, I'm just thinking about my to-do list for the NAACP.

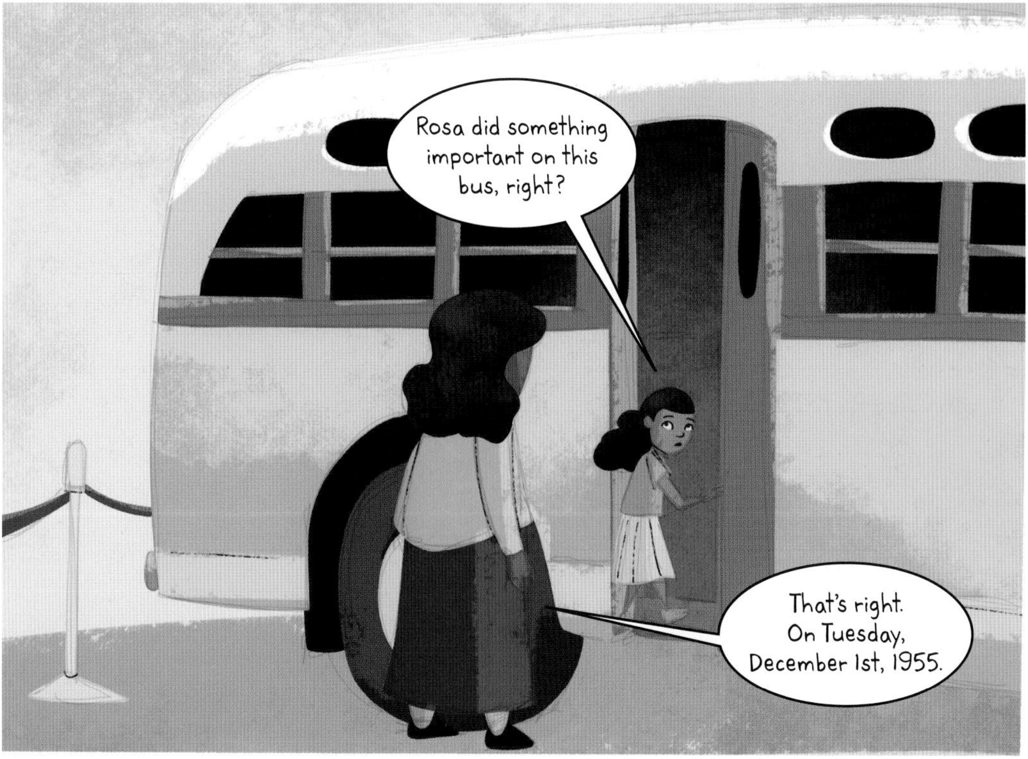
Rosa did something important on this bus, right?
That's right. On Tuesday, December 1st, 1955.

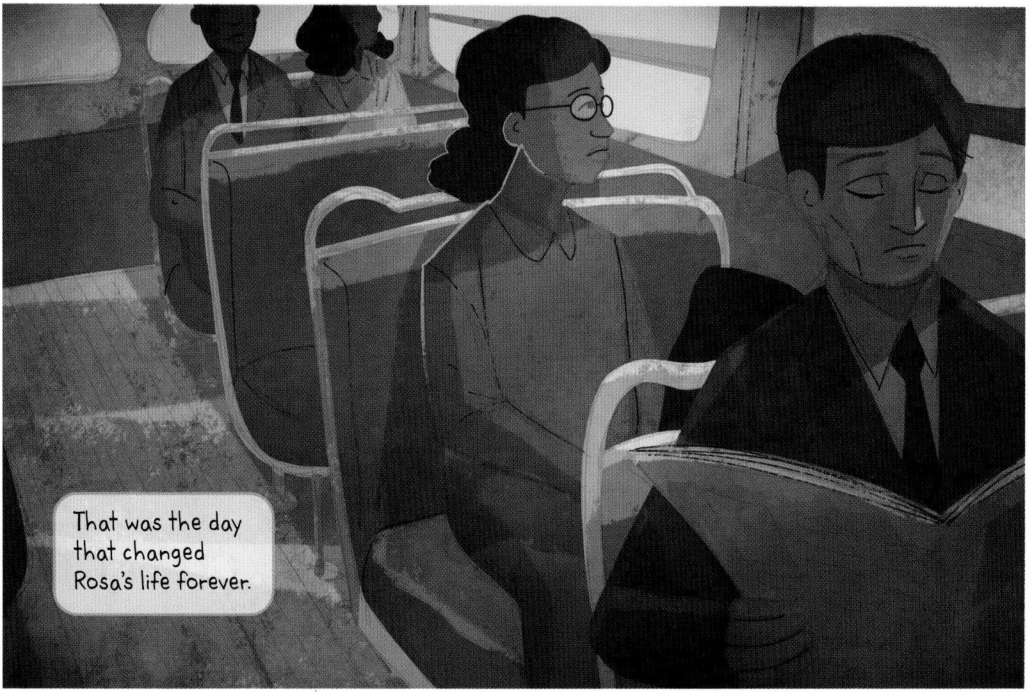
That was the day that changed Rosa's life forever.

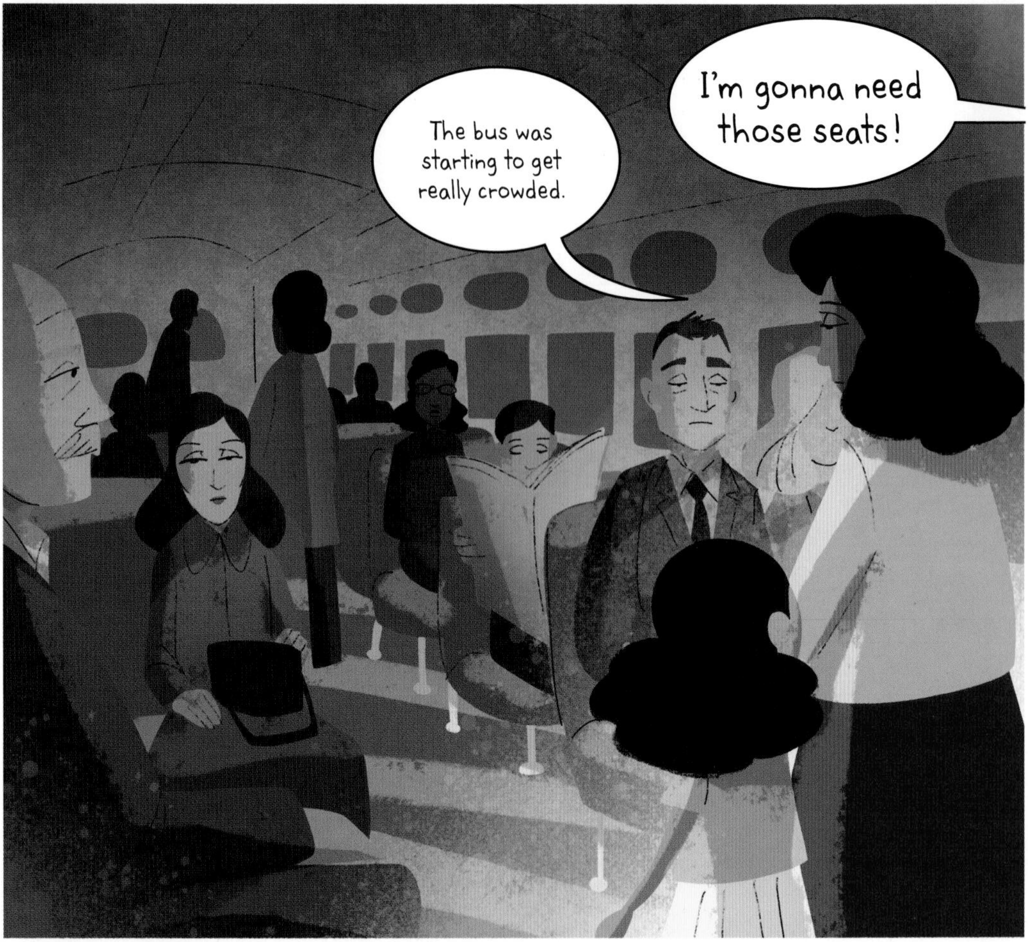
The bus was starting to get really crowded.
I'm gonna need those seats!

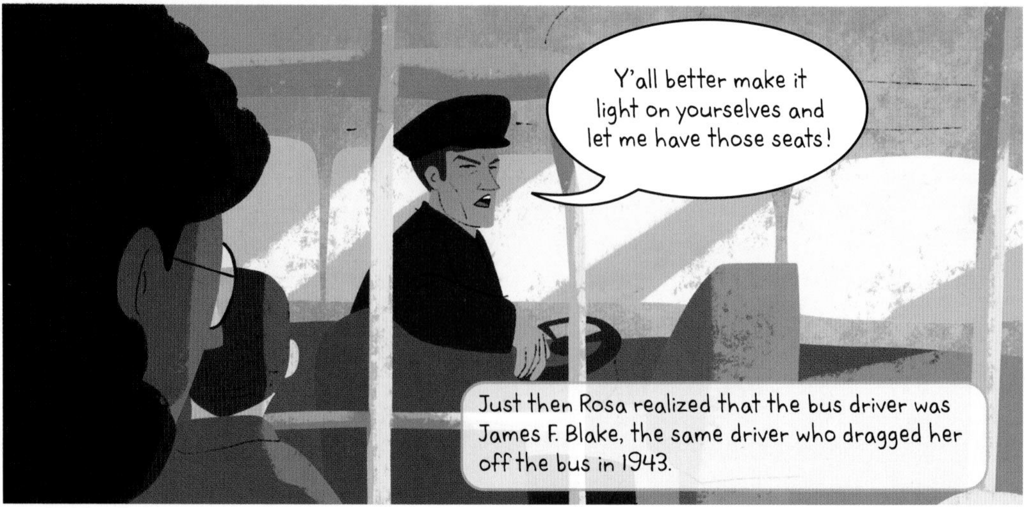
Y'all better make it light on yourselves and let me have those seats!
Just then Rosa realized that the bus driver was James F. Blake, the same driver who dragged her off the bus in 1943.

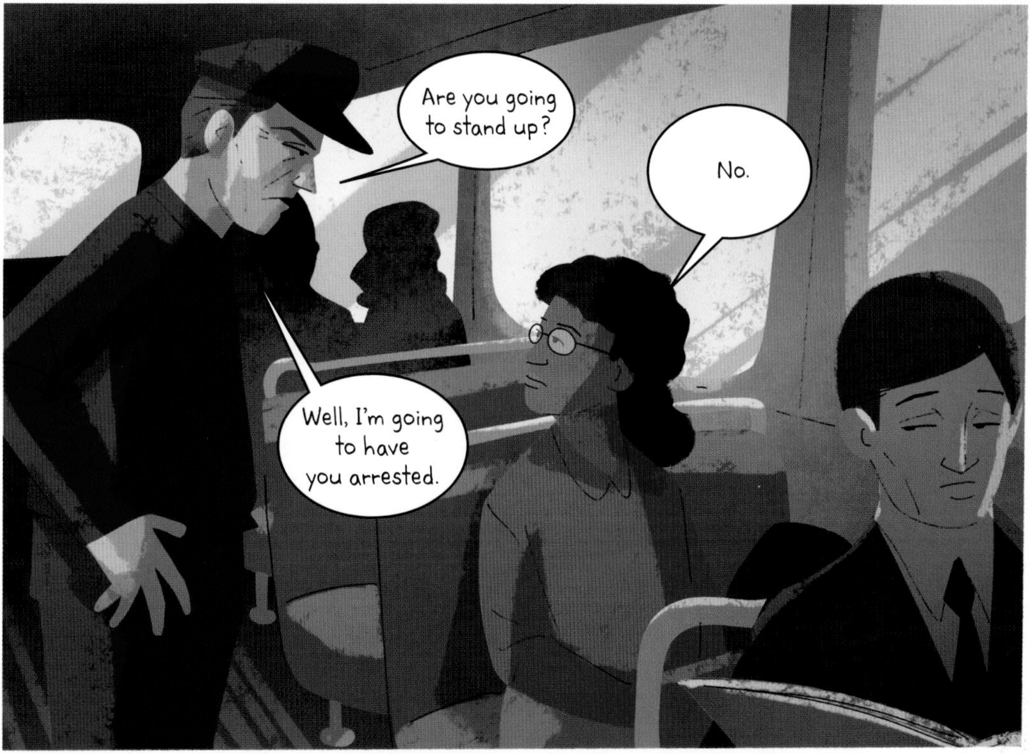
Are you going to stand up?
No.
Well, I'm going to have you arrested.

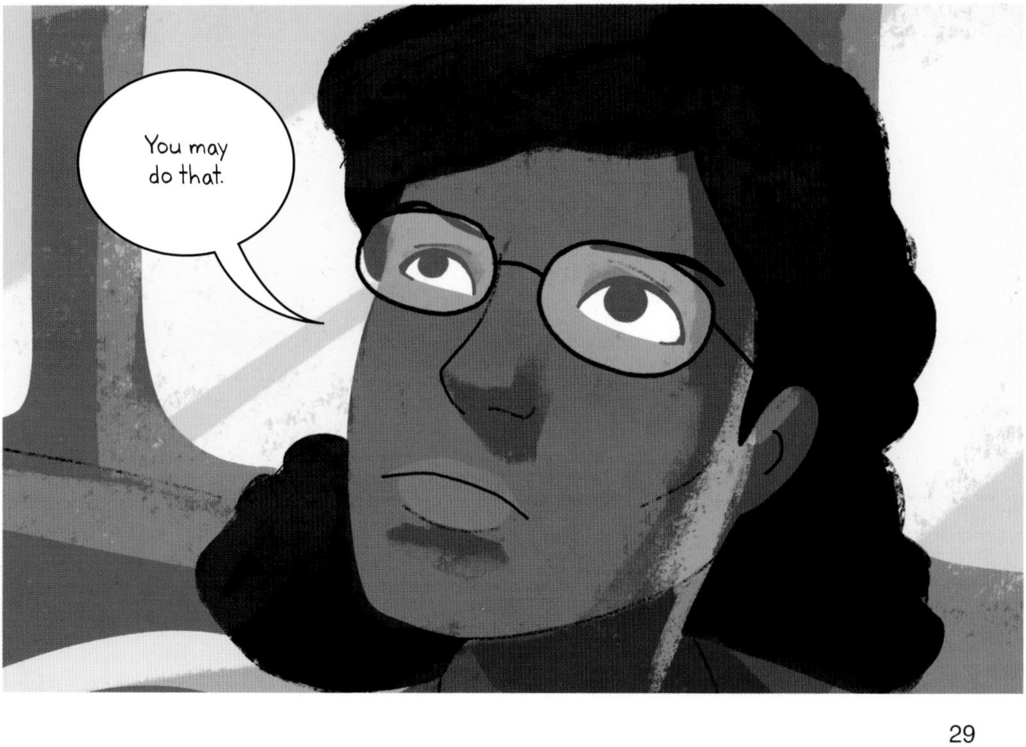
You may do that.

"People always say that I didn't give up my seat because I was tired, but that isn't true. No, the only tired I was, was tired of giving in."

—Rosa Parks

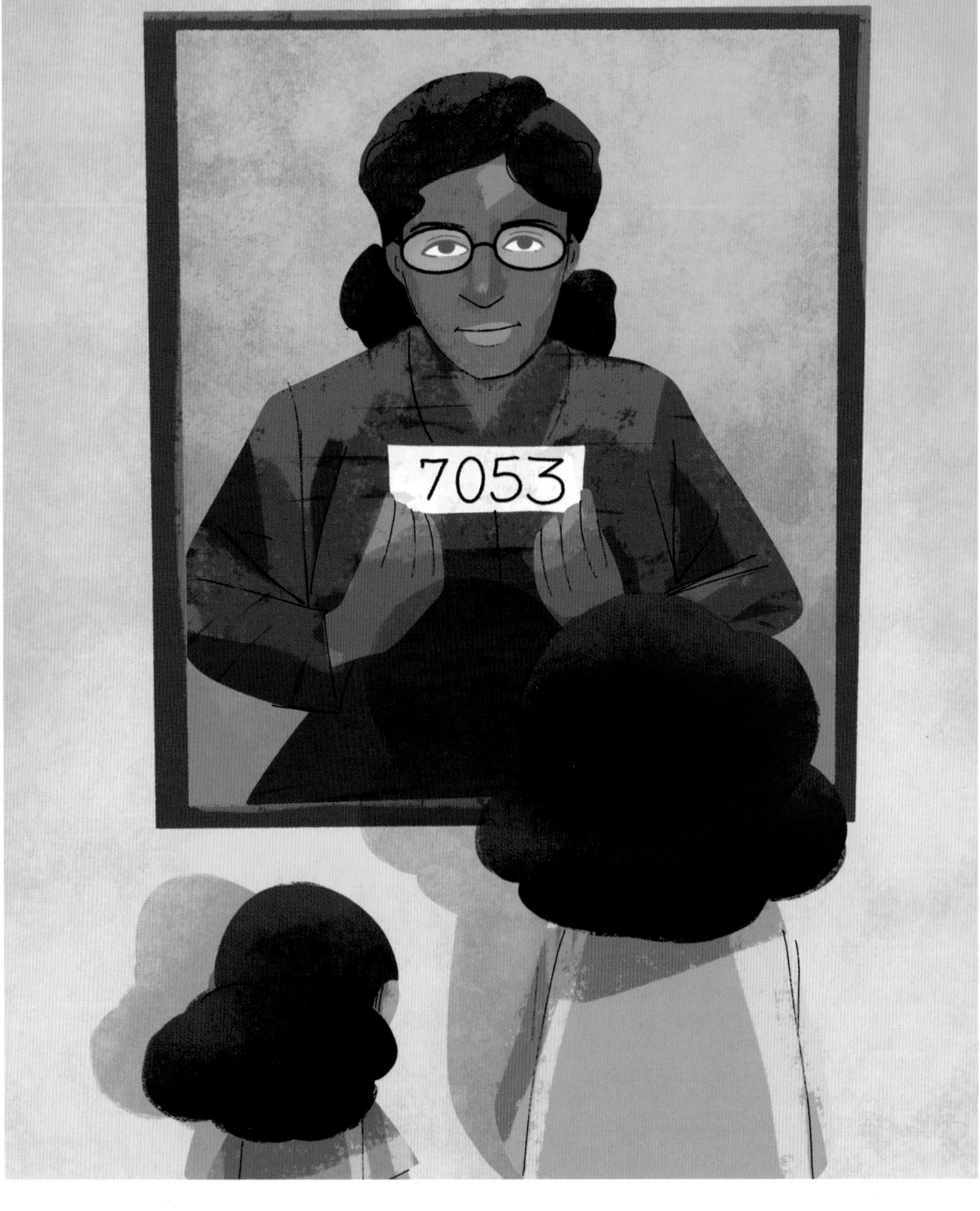
7053

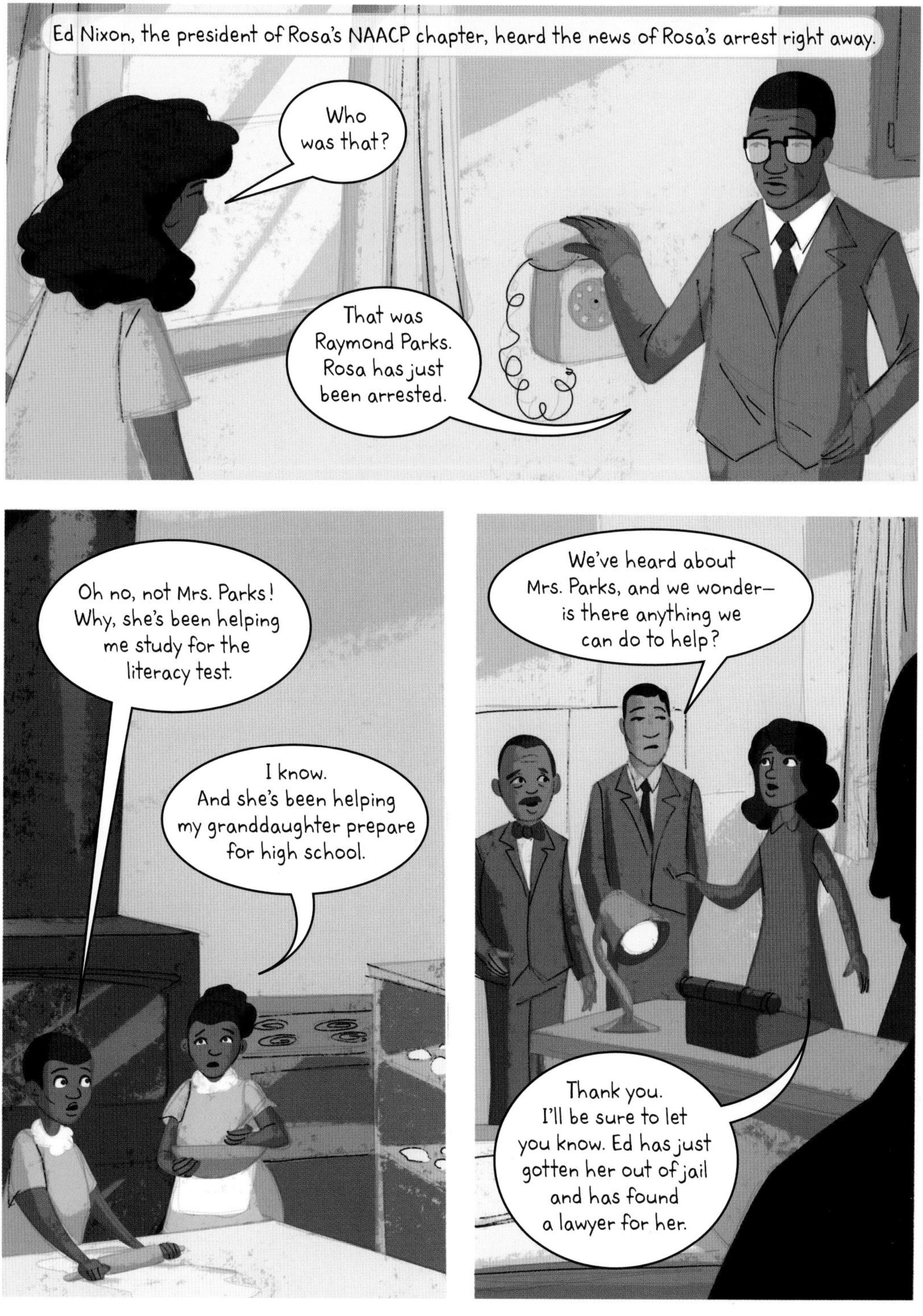

Ed Nixon, the president of Rosa's NAACP chapter, heard the news of Rosa's arrest right away.
Who was that?
That was Raymond Parks. Rosa has just been arrested.
Oh no, not Mrs. Parks! Why, she's been helping me study for the literacy test.
I know. And she's been helping my granddaughter prepare for high school.
We've heard about Mrs. Parks, and we wonder— is there anything we can do to help?
Thank you. I'll be sure to let you know. Ed has just gotten her out of jail and has found a lawyer for her.

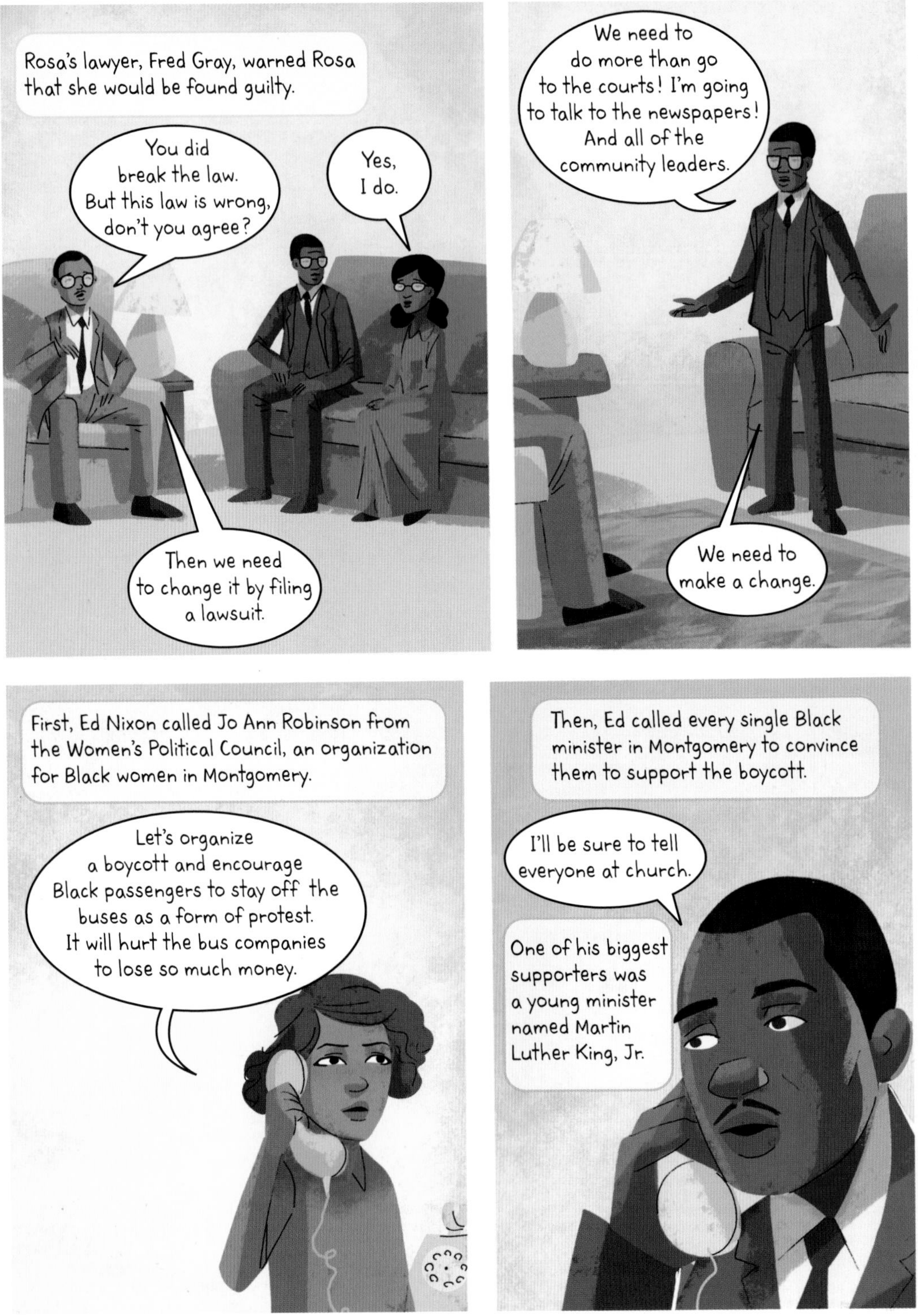
Rosa's lawyer, Fred Gray, warned Rosa that she would be found guilty.
You did break the law. But this law is wrong, don't you agree?
Yes, I do.
Then we need to change it by filing a lawsuit.
We need to do more than go to the courts! I'm going to talk to the newspapers! And all of the community leaders.
We need to make a change.
First, Ed Nixon called Jo Ann Robinson from the Women's Political Council, an organization for Black women in Montgomery.
Let's organize a boycott and encourage Black passengers to stay off the buses as a form of protest. It will hurt the bus companies to lose so much money.
Then, Ed called every single Black minister in Montgomery to convince them to support the boycott.
I'll be sure to tell everyone at church.
One of his biggest supporters was a young minister named Martin Luther King, Jr.

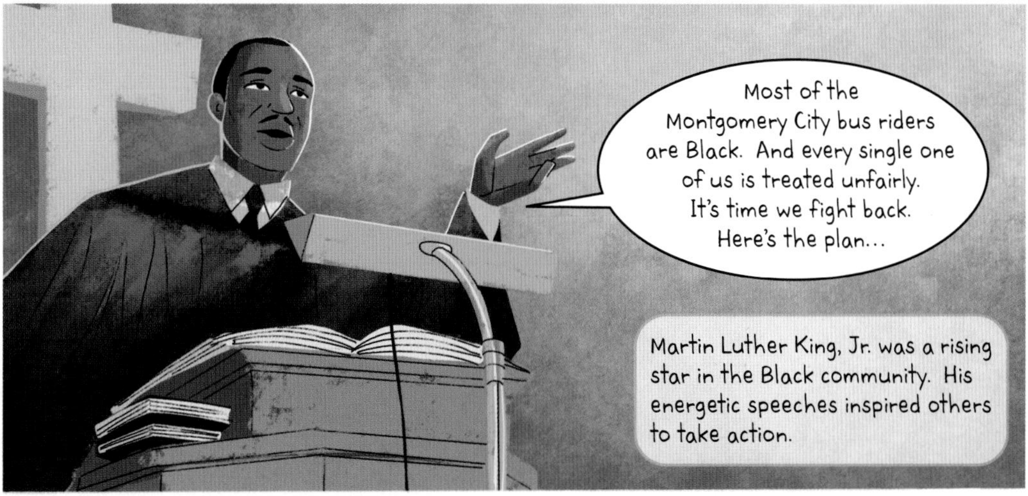
Most of the Montgomery City bus riders are Black. And every single one of us is treated unfairly. It's time we fight back. Here's the plan...
Martin Luther King, Jr. was a rising star in the Black community. His energetic speeches inspired others to take action.

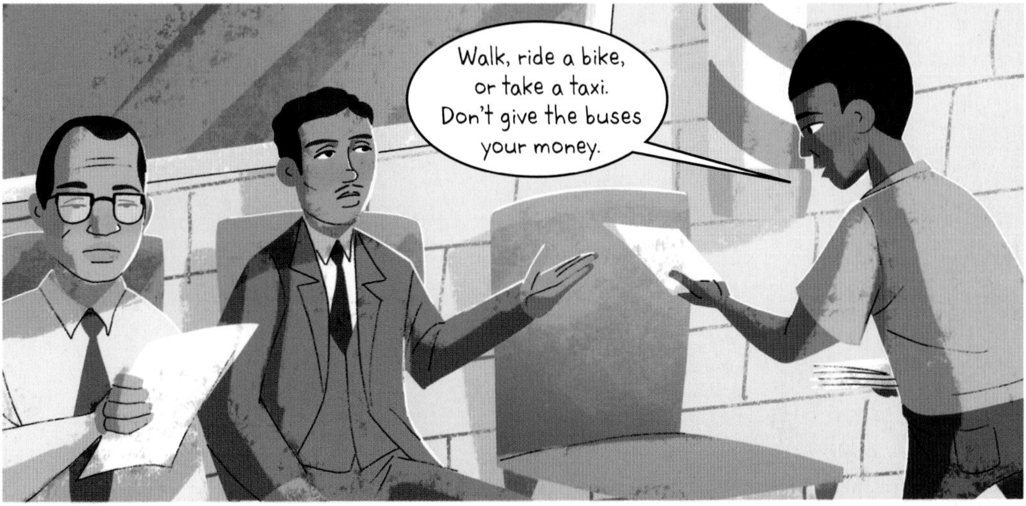
Walk, ride a bike, or take a taxi. Don't give the buses your money.

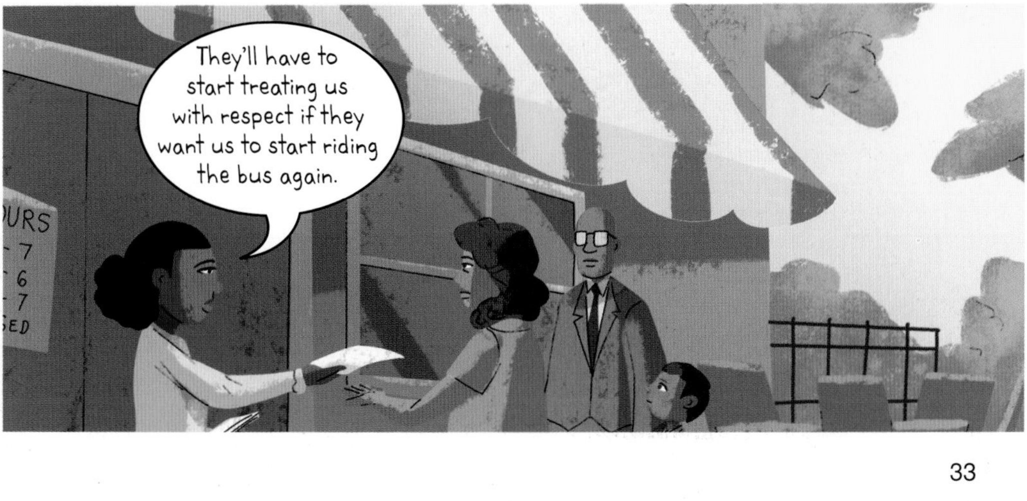
They'll have to start treating us with respect if they want us to start riding the bus again.

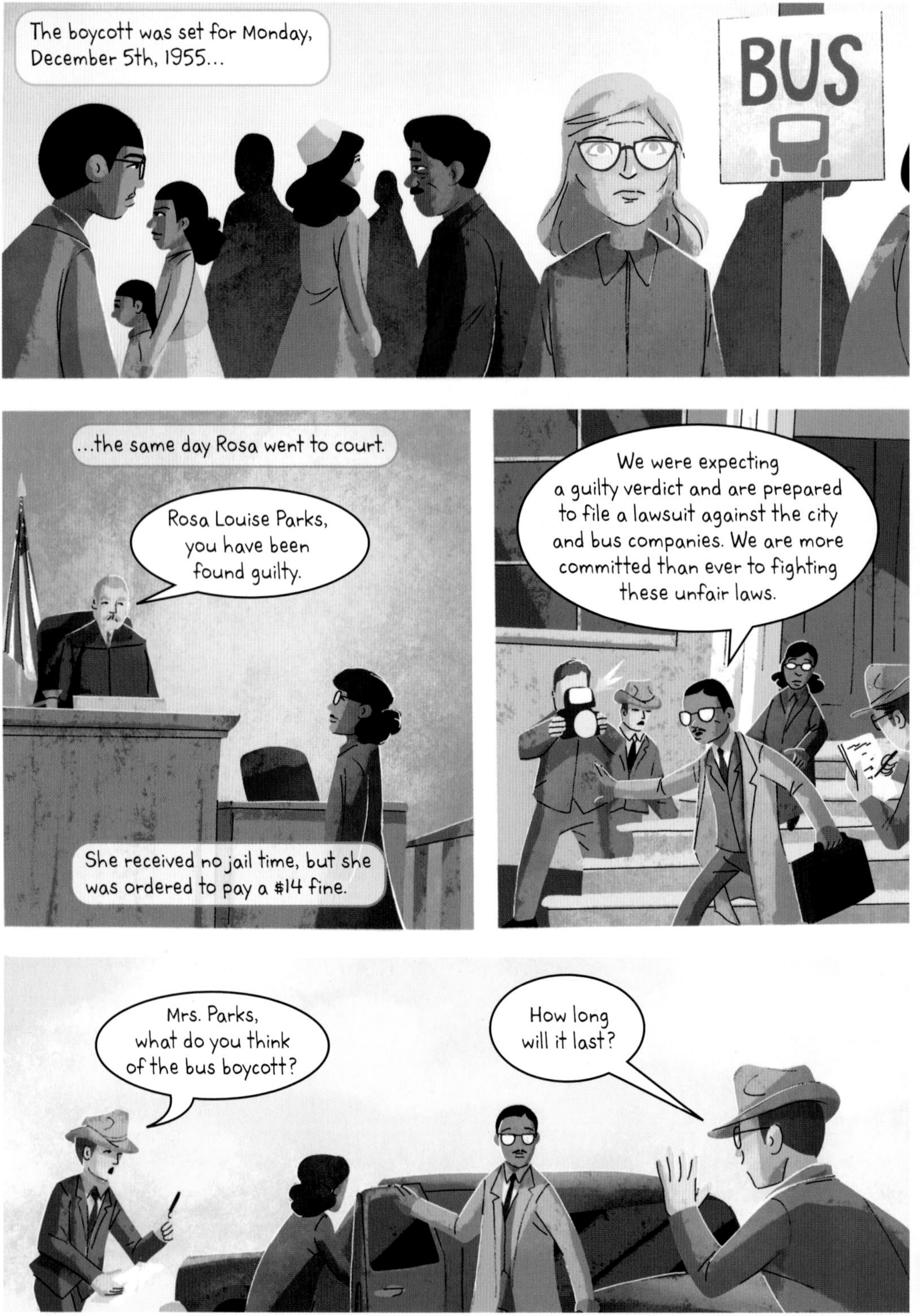
The boycott was set for Monday, December 5th, 1955...
BUS
...the same day Rosa went to court.
Rosa Louise Parks, you have been found guilty.
She received no jail time, but she was ordered to pay a $14 fine.
We were expecting a guilty verdict and are prepared to file a lawsuit against the city and bus companies. We are more committed than ever to fighting these unfair laws.
Mrs. Parks, what do you think of the bus boycott?
How long will it last?

We demanded that the city and bus companies hire Black drivers and end bus segregation, but they just laughed at us.

Then we won't ride the buses until they take us seriously. We'll rent vans and be our own bus company!

The Montgomery bus boycott was supposed to last one day. It continued for 13 months.

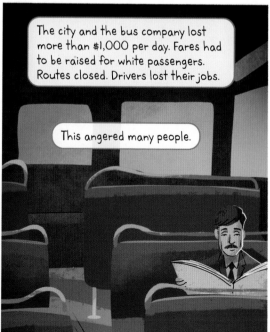

The city and the bus company lost more than $1,000 per day. Fares had to be raised for white passengers. Routes closed. Drivers lost their jobs.

This angered many people.

The boycott leaders were threatened, bullied, and arrested. Rosa and Parks even lost their jobs.

But they weren't discouraged.

We'll find a way.

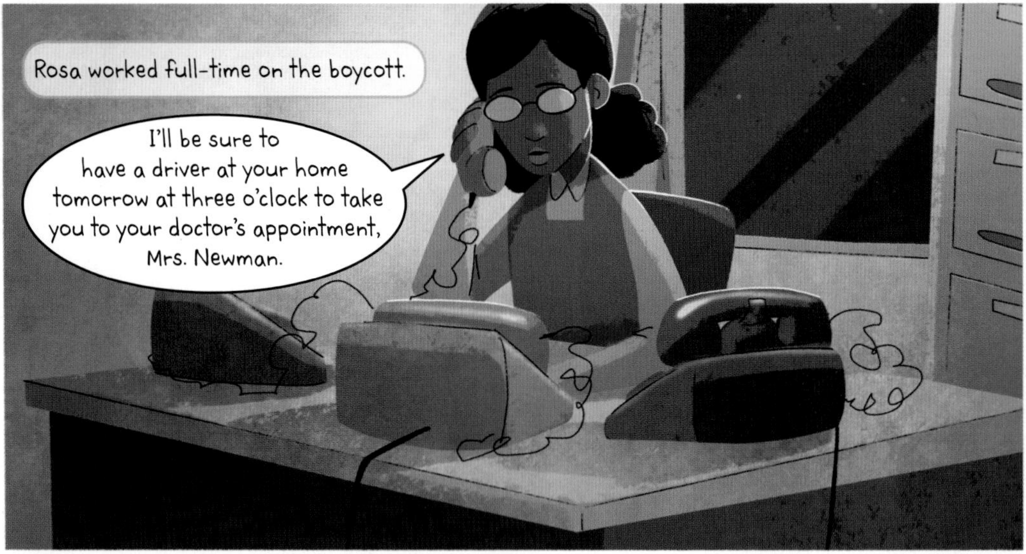
Rosa worked full-time on the boycott.
I'll be sure to have a driver at your home tomorrow at three o'clock to take you to your doctor's appointment, Mrs. Newman.

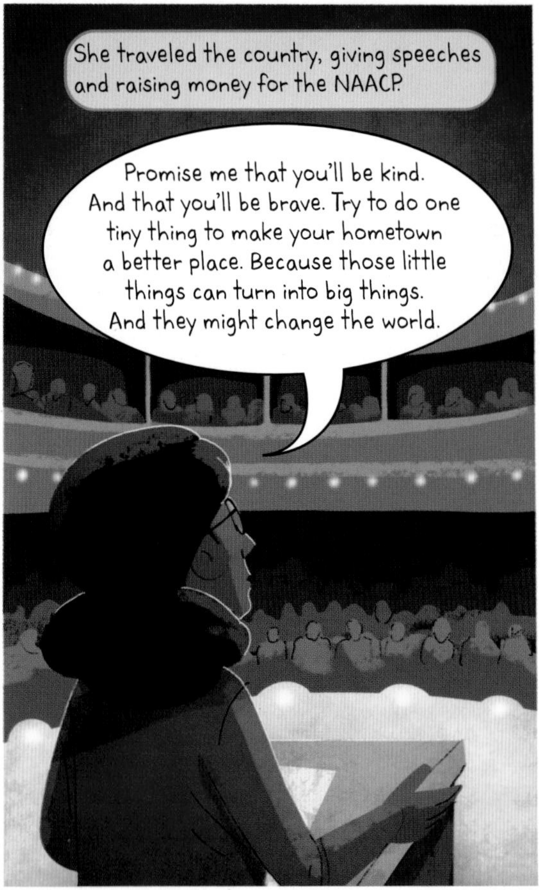
She traveled the country, giving speeches and raising money for the NAACP.
Promise me that you'll be kind. And that you'll be brave. Try to do one tiny thing to make your hometown a better place. Because those little things can turn into big things. And they might change the world.

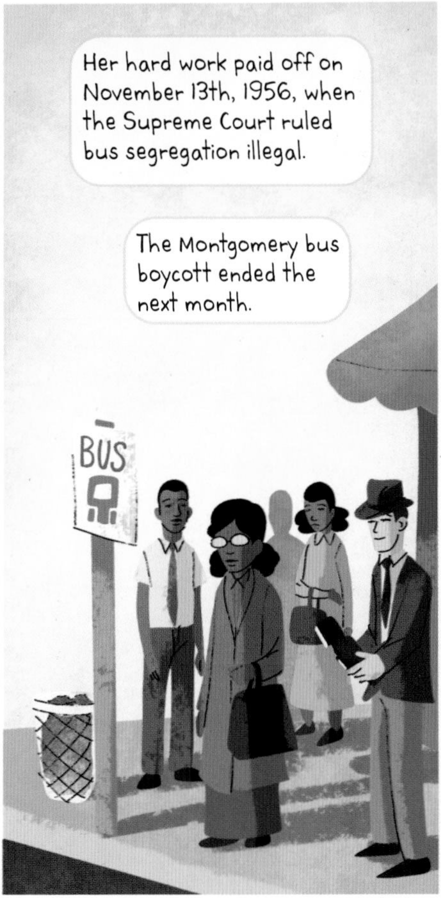
Her hard work paid off on November 13th, 1956, when the Supreme Court ruled bus segregation illegal.
The Montgomery bus boycott ended the next month.
BUS

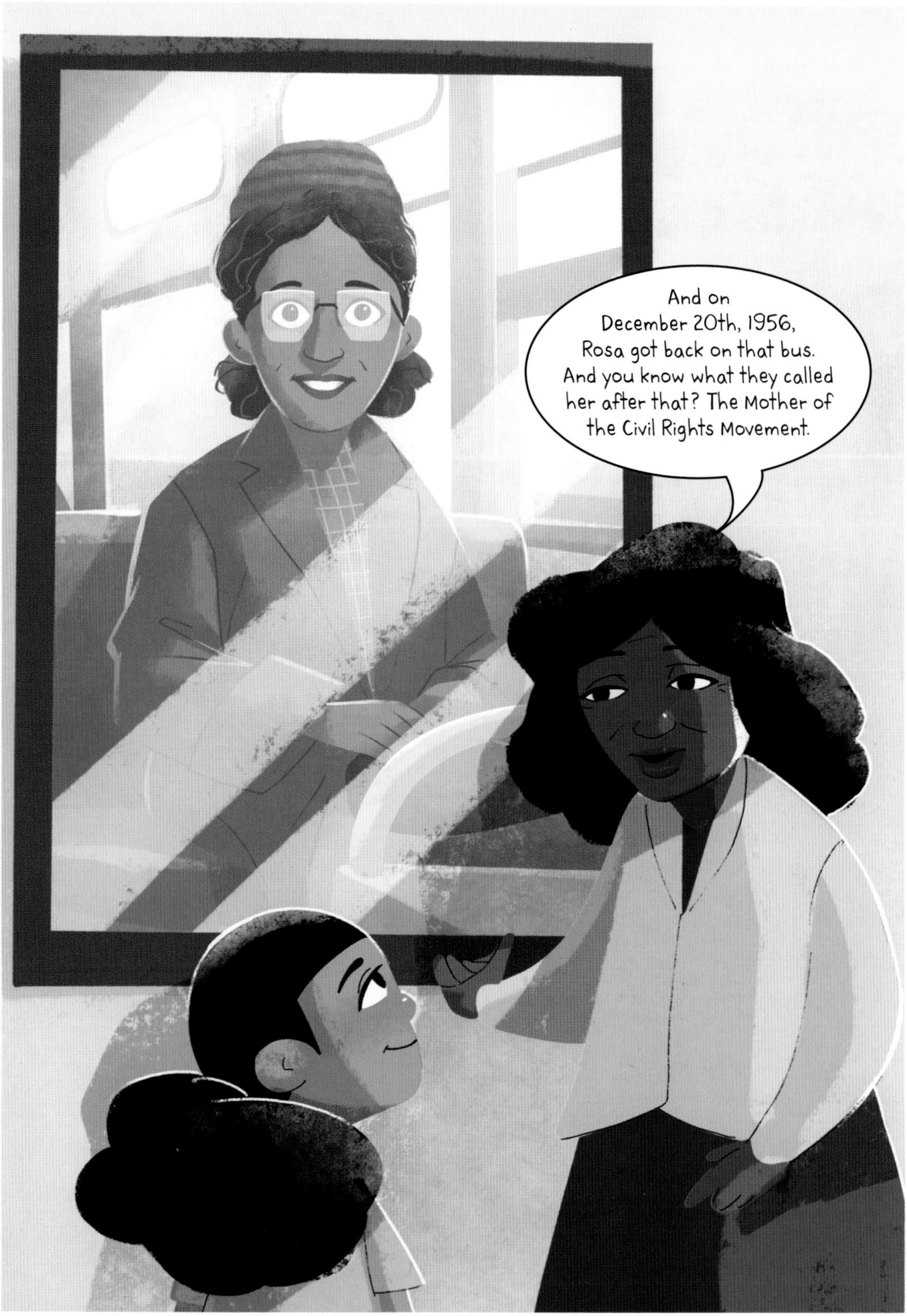
And on
December 20th, 1956,
Rosa got back on that bus.
And you know what they called
her after that? The Mother of
the Civil Rights Movement.

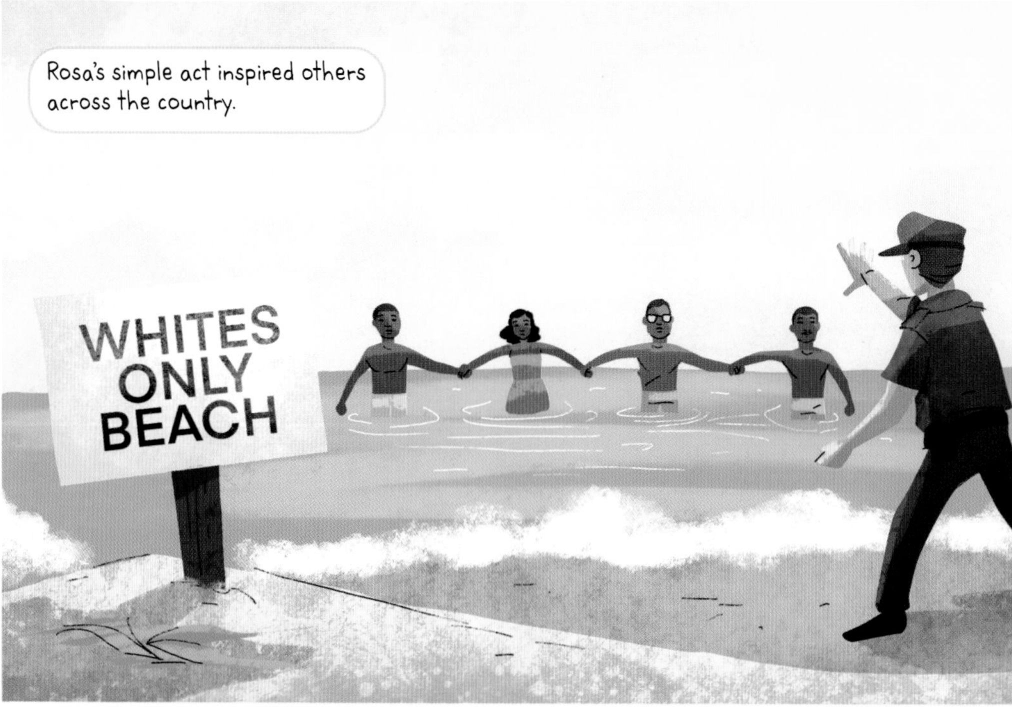
Rosa's simple act inspired others across the country.
WHITES ONLY BEACH

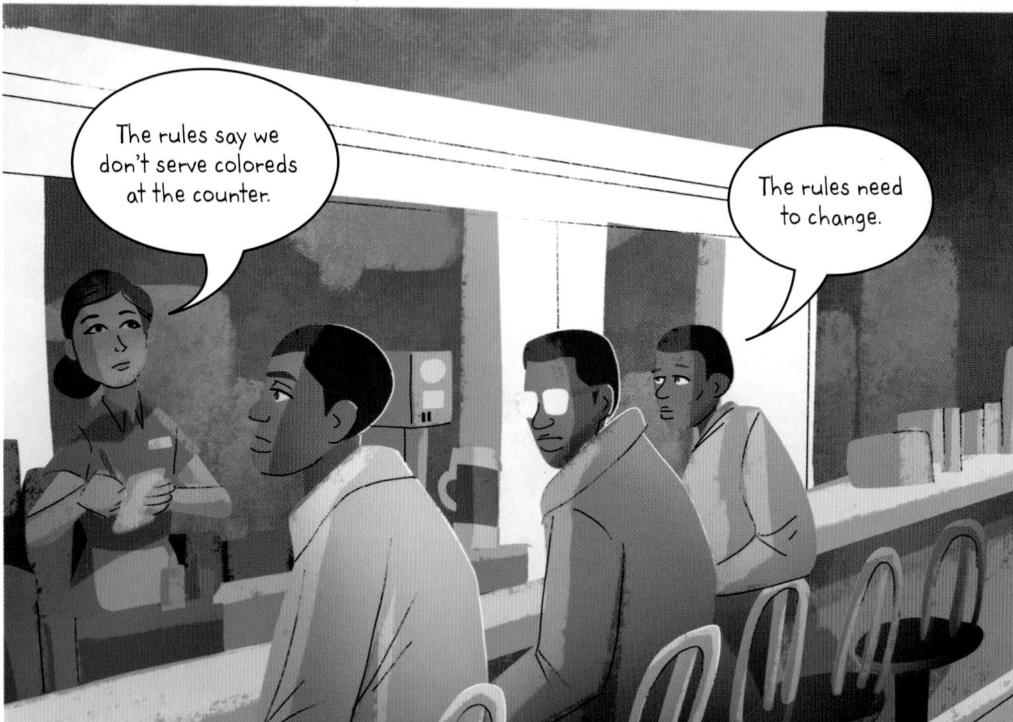
The rules say we don't serve coloreds at the counter.
The rules need to change.

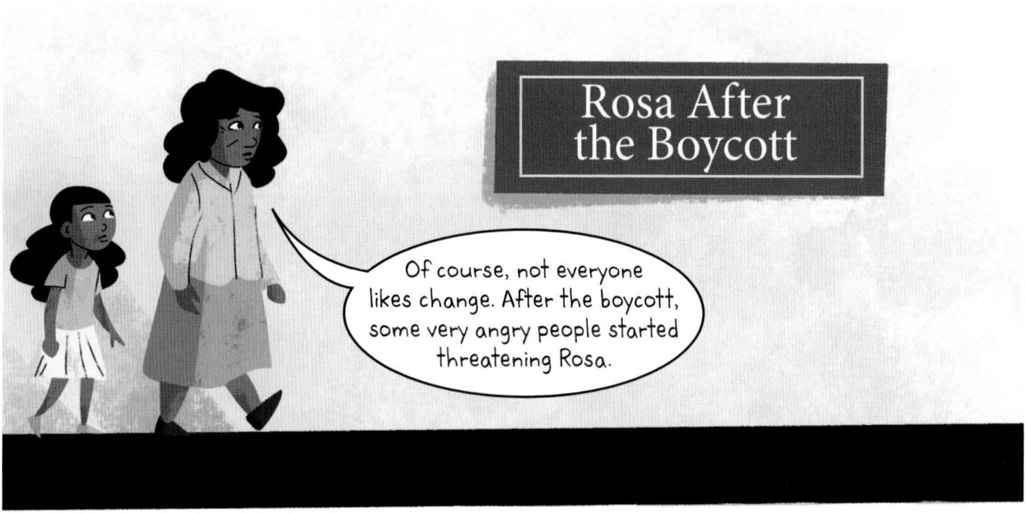
Rosa After the Boycott
Of course, not everyone likes change. After the boycott, some very angry people started threatening Rosa.

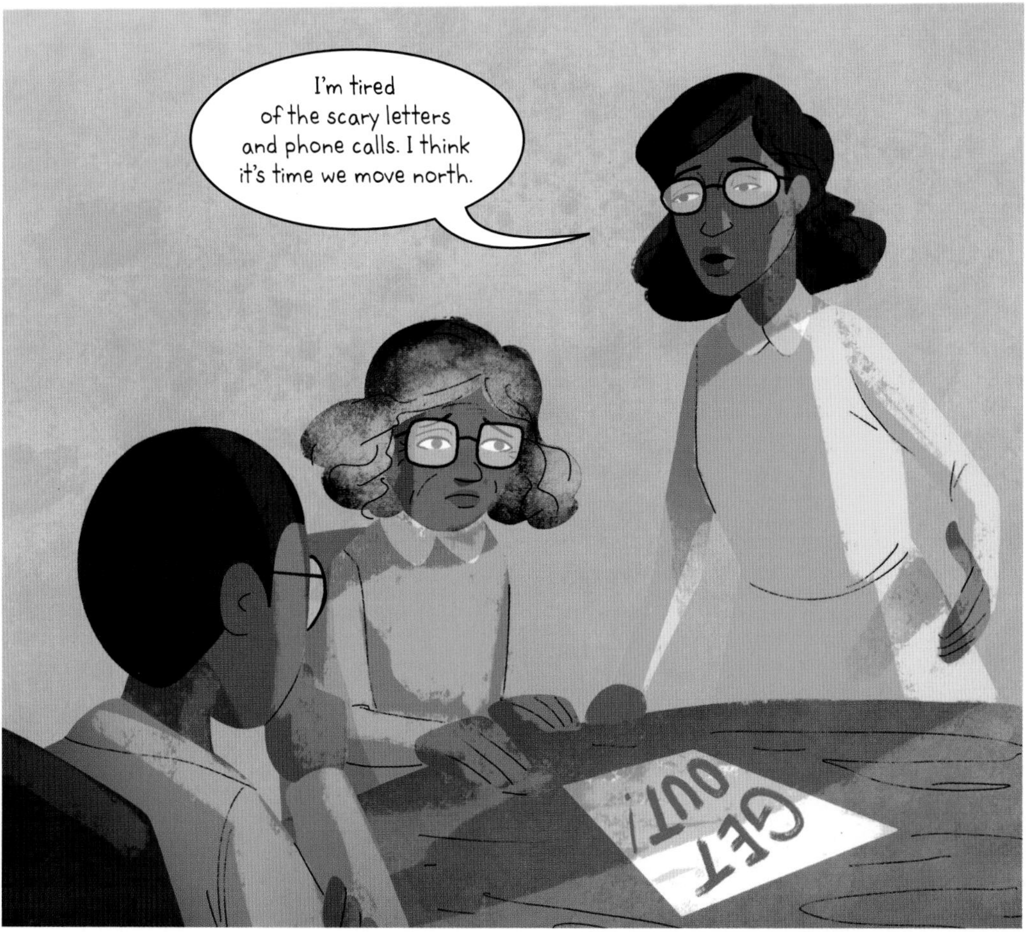
I'm tired of the scary letters and phone calls. I think it's time we move north.
GET OUT!

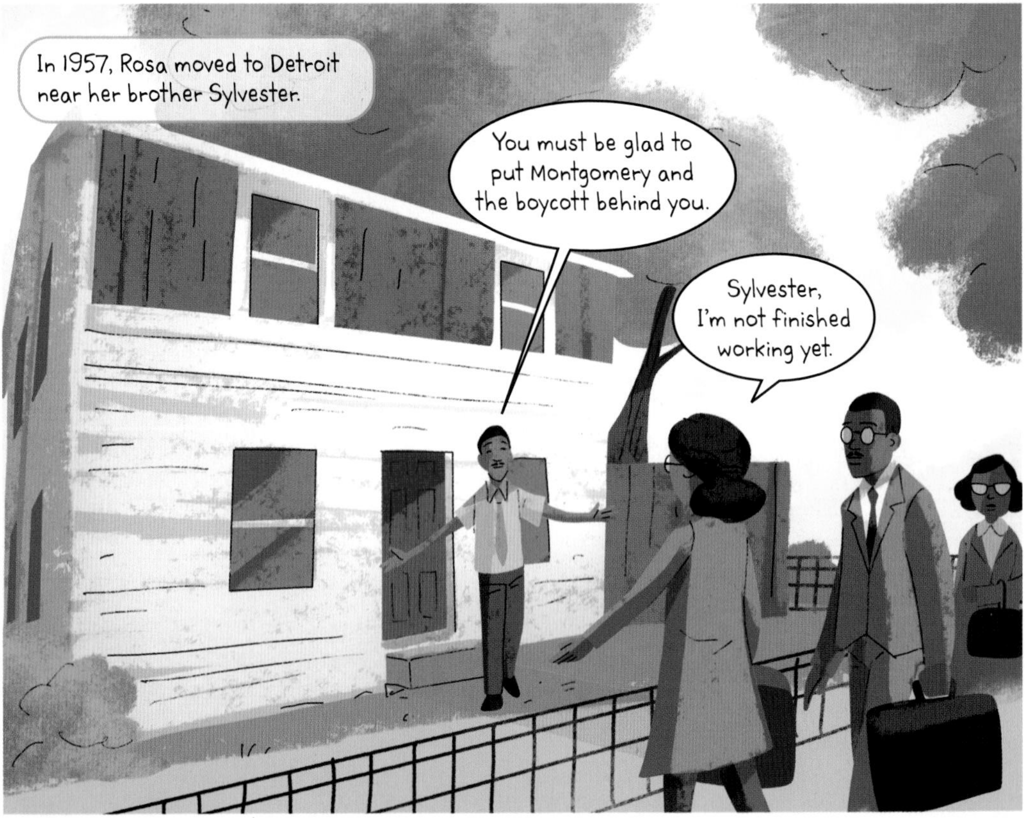
In 1957, Rosa moved to Detroit near her brother Sylvester.
You must be glad to put Montgomery and the boycott behind you.
Sylvester, I'm not finished working yet.

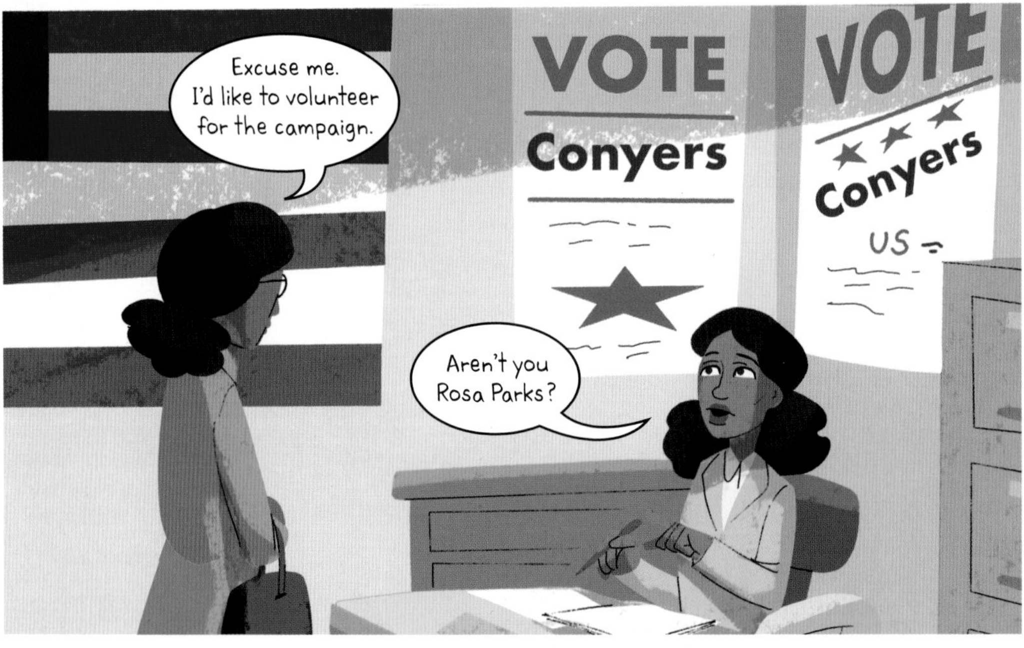
Excuse me. I'd like to volunteer for the campaign.
VOTE
Conyers
VOTE
Conyers
US
Aren't you Rosa Parks?

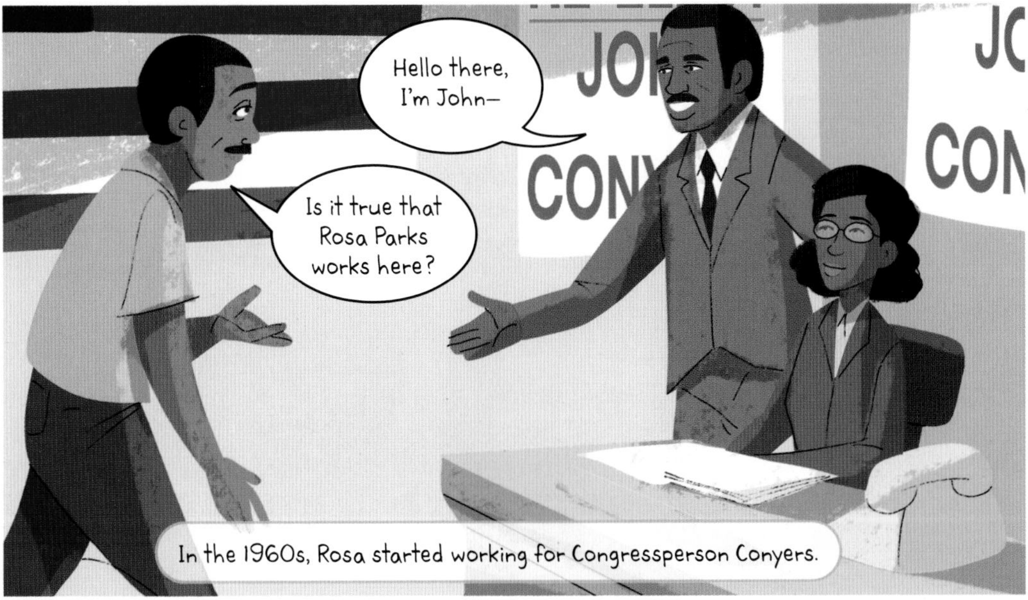
Hello there, I'm John—
Is it true that Rosa Parks works here?
In the 1960s, Rosa started working for Congressperson Conyers.

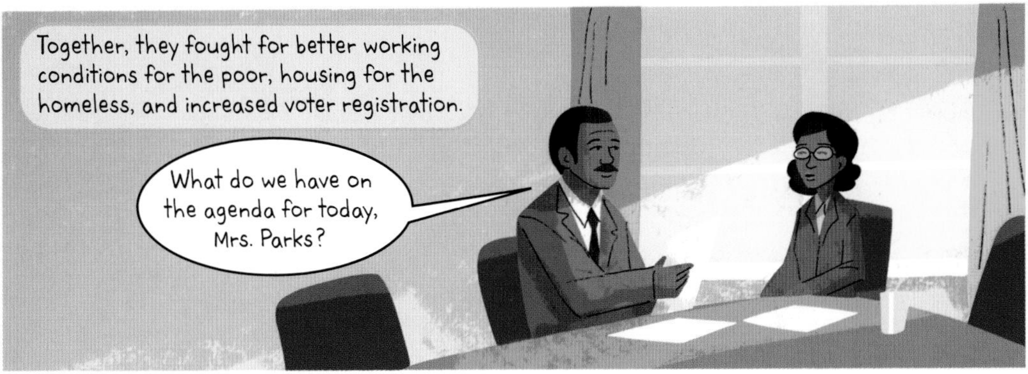
Together, they fought for better working conditions for the poor, housing for the homeless, and increased voter registration.
What do we have on the agenda for today, Mrs. Parks?

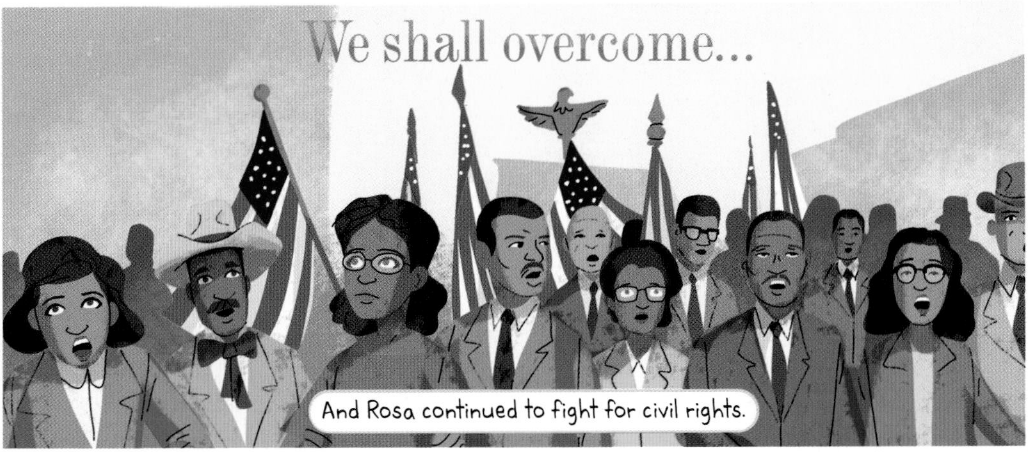
We shall overcome...
And Rosa continued to fight for civil rights.

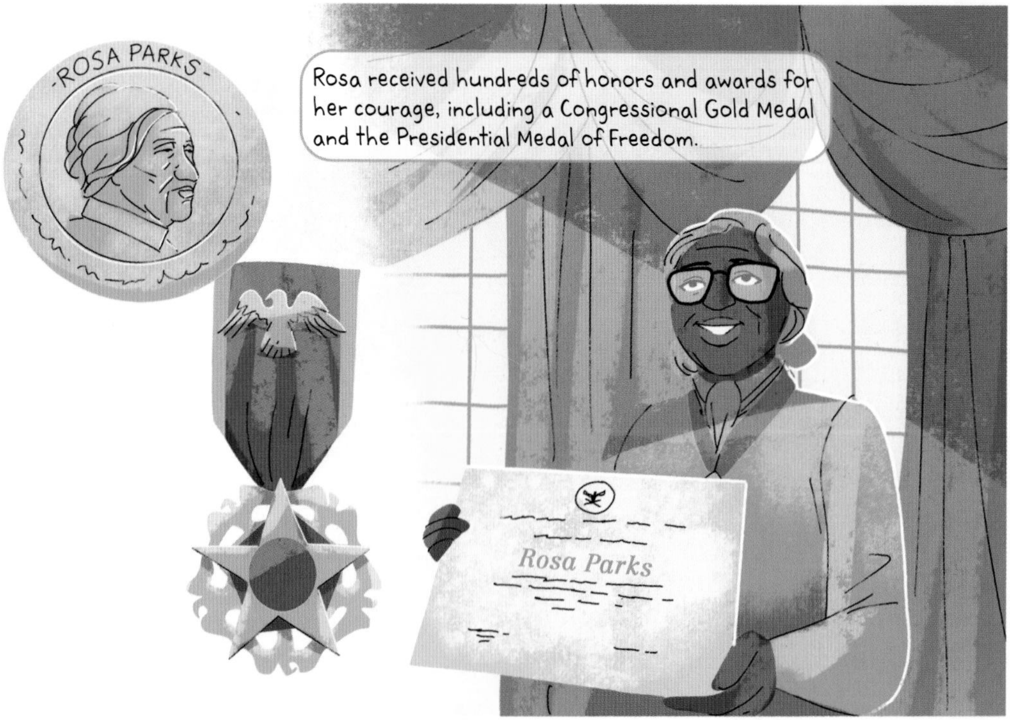
ROSA PARKS
Rosa received hundreds of honors and awards for her courage, including a Congressional Gold Medal and the Presidential Medal of Freedom.
Rosa Parks

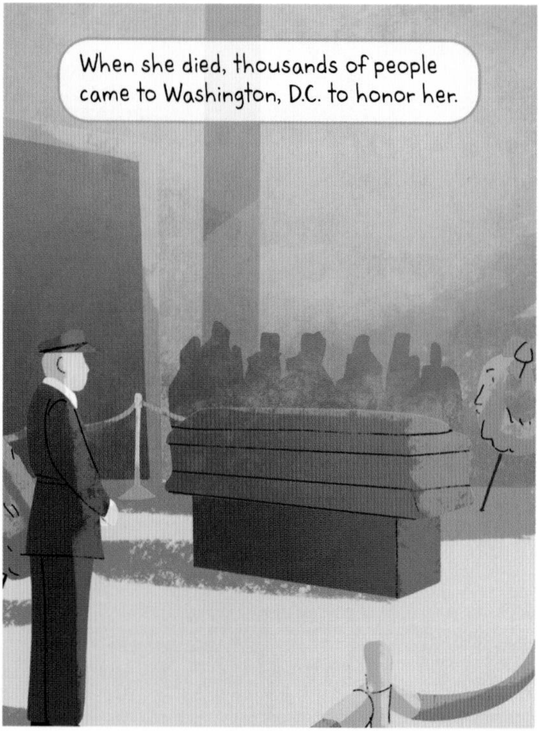
When she died, thousands of people came to Washington, D.C. to honor her.

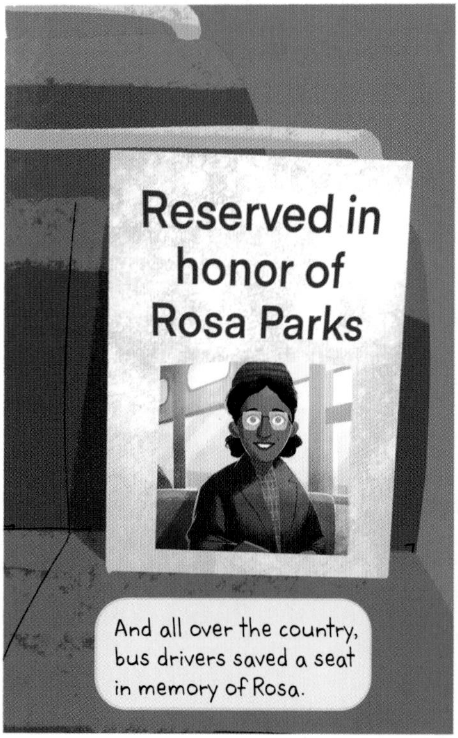
Reserved in honor of Rosa Parks
And all over the country, bus drivers saved a seat in memory of Rosa.

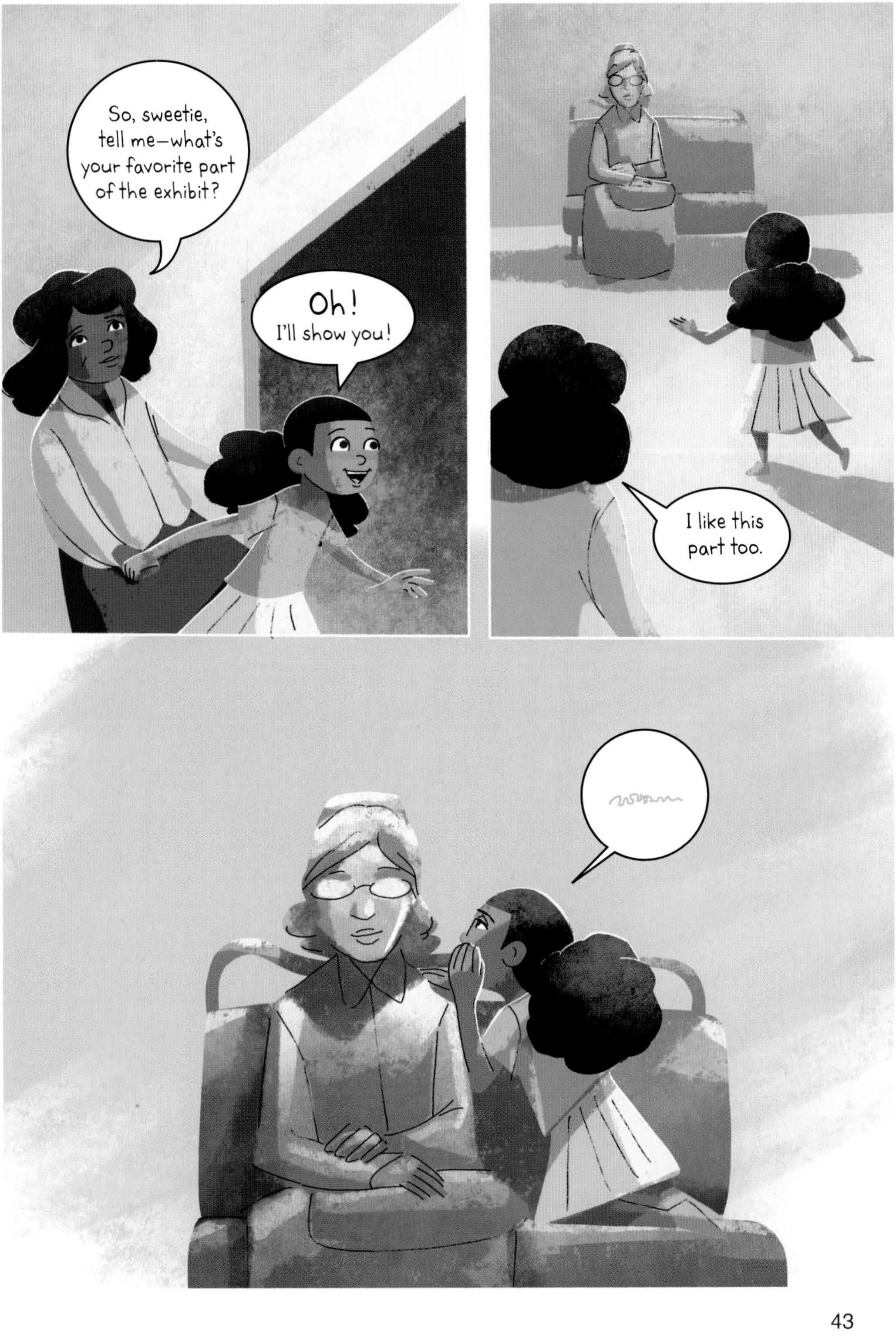
So, sweetie, tell me—what's your favorite part of the exhibit?
Oh! I'll show you!
I like this part too.

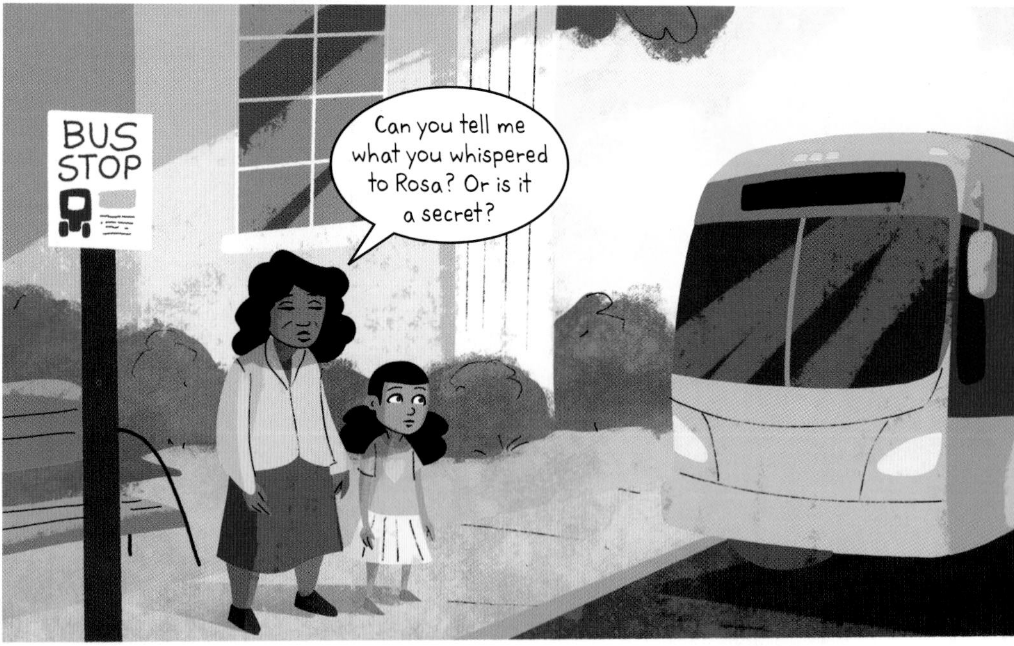
BUS STOP
Can you tell me what you whispered to Rosa? Or is it a secret?

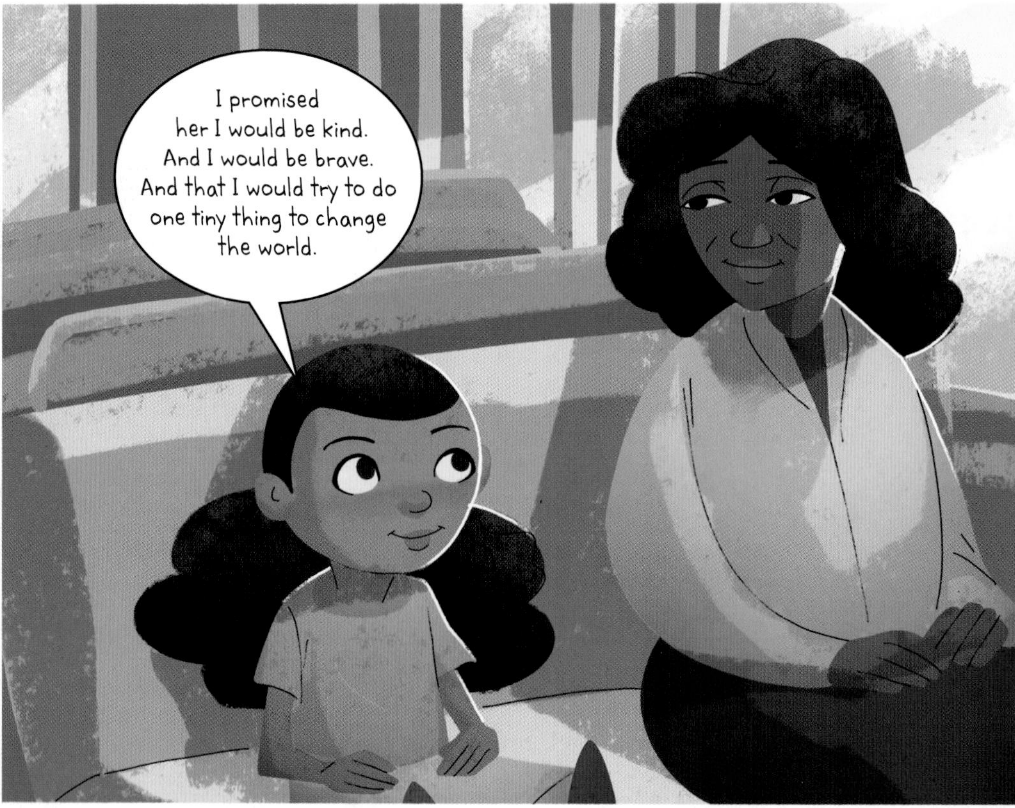
I promised her I would be kind. And I would be brave. And that I would try to do one tiny thing to change the world.

Lauren Burke is a writer and podcaster from Chicago, Illinois. Her work focuses on women's history, writing, and travel. Her book **Why She Wrote** is due in 2021.

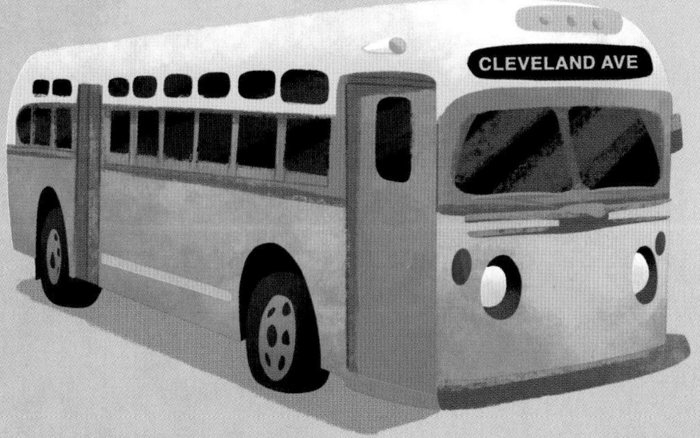
CLEVELAND AVE

Largely self-taught, **Shane Clester** initially worked in comics and storyboards. He has transitioned to his real passion—children's books—even self-publishing several of his own. He currently lives in Florida with his wonderful wife and their two kids.

Also available:

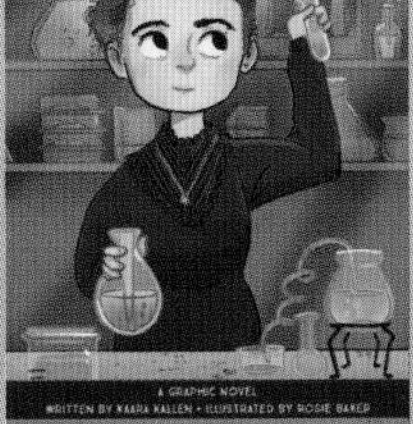
IT'S HER STORY
MARIE CURIE
A GRAPHIC NOVEL

"Each person must live their
life as a model for others."